Fred W. McDarrah

was born in Brooklyn in 1926. He was in the paratroops during his Army service from 1944–1947, and in 1954 he graduated from New York University. His first published photograph appeared in *The Village Voice*, February, 1959. In 1962 he became the *Voice* Staff Photographer. So far he has won six press photography competitions for the *Voice*, three of which were first-place awards.

Fred McDarrah's published books include *The Beat Scene* (1960); *The Artist's World* (1961); *Greenwich Village* (1963); *New York, New York* (1964); and a collaboration, *The New Bohemia* (1966). His photographs and picture stories have appeared in *Art News, Arts Magazine, Esquire, Evergreen Review, Life, The New York Times Magazine, New York (World Journal Tribune), Newsweek, Pageant, Progressive Architecture, Status/Diplomat, Toronto Star, Time,* and *The Urban Review.*

Some of Mr. McDarrah's photographs have been converted into wall-size personality posters celebrating such popular heroes as Bob Dylan, Allen Ginsberg, Senator Robert F. Kennedy, Dr. Timothy Leary, Jean Shepherd, and Andy Warhol.

"Let us look at the art museum not as a collection of tangible artifacts, but rather as an expression of ideas and feelings about man and his most important work—art."

—Albert Ten Eyck Gardner

Museums
in New York

A descriptive reference guide to
seventy-nine fine arts museums, local history
museums, specialized museums, natural
history and science museums, libraries,
botanical and zoological parks, commercial
collections, and historic houses and
mansions open to the public within the five
boroughs of New York City

Text and 200 photographs
by FRED W. MC DARRAH

FOREWORD BY THOMAS P. F. HOVING
Director, The Metropolitan Museum of Art

E. P. DUTTON & CO., INC. New York
1967

*A Dutton
Paperback*

*Frontispiece: In a garden at The Cloisters,
with the George Washington Bridge
in the background.*

*facing page 8: Human head of a winged lion
guarding an entrance to the palace of Ashurnasirpal II,
King of Assyria (883–859* B.C.*), at Kalhu (modern Nimrud).
Now to be seen at the Metropolitan Museum of Art.*

———————————

For Timothy and Jonathan

Foreword

There are plenty of guidebooks in the world. There are even a lot of guidebooks to New York. Some of these guidebooks are very good on logistics, or photographs, or descriptions, or any number of other things. This one is good for all of these purposes. It is a guide for museums, mansions, and mausoleums. If any of these venerable institutions captures your fancy, this is the book for you.

The guidebook can be used by any sort of New Yorker. For those who have ventured to the far corners of the City in quest of their heritage, this book will be a reminder that they have nevertheless not seen all there is to see. For those who have never ventured beyond the big mammas of New York museums, the Metropolitan or the Modern, this book will give a warning that a lot is left to be seen.

Things to be seen are made very attractive by the photographs, which capture moods and ambiances so perfectly. Sometimes perhaps too revealingly perfect. But it is good that way, because you will have to find out for yourself what the best things in New York are. And you are tantalized to do so by the photography.

It has long been known to New Yorkers that there is more to the City than they suspect. There is more for children to do than to gloat morbidly over mummies, however delightful that may be. There is more local history encased between the skyscrapers than even the most fervent students of New York suspect. And there are more subway lines than anyone has ever ventured on, to take you to just these little lonely places. Everything is explained in this book—the reasons for going, the how-to-go, and the what-to-expect.

One word about the biggest reason for going to any museum. Presumably, you are relatively aware of your daily surroundings. If you are also a bit curious as to how it is that your life runs along particular lines, and that you are surrounded by particular objects, and that certain things seem beautiful to you—if you are just a bit curious about the condition of man—then you are a museum person. Not every day, but every once in a while you feel like seeing something other than your four walls. These are the times that you go to a museum.

So swing yourself into a subway and explore, and as reassurance, take along this guide.

THOMAS P. F. HOVING

Contents

12 |

| 13

Museums In New York

AMERICAN MUSEUM OF IMMIGRATION
Address: Liberty Island, New York, N.Y.
Phone: RE 2-1286

Days: Open daily, 9–5; open till 6 in summer.
Admission: Free.

Ferry: Leaves Battery Park landing for Liberty Island every hour on
  the hour. Round trip fare: Adults $.90, Children $.40.
Subway: IRT 7th Ave. or Lexington Ave. to South Ferry station.
Bus: Broadway bus to South Ferry.
Auto: South to Bowling Green and State St. No cars on Liberty
  Island ferries. Public parking lots and meters at Battery Park.

Restaurant: Snack bar, vending machines near ferry dock.

The American Museum of Immigration is scheduled to open soon
under the administration of the National Park Service of the United
States Department of the Interior. It is being built on twelve-acre
Liberty Island, at the base of the Statue of Liberty, the first symbol of
democracy visible to immigrants at the threshold of the New World.
Up to this time the 150-foot-high female figure of Liberty enlighten-
ing the world stood amid the remains of Fort Wood.

The museum will be situated in a star-shaped rampart. Four exhibit
halls will be at the center. Each of the ten sections of the rampart
will house a separate arm of the museum: auditorium, study collection,
workrooms, library, hall of records, etc. The changing exhibit area
will be devoted to the innumerable contributions of the immigrants | 17
to the building of America. Contributions to the fields of invention,
engineering, science, art, music, industry, and crafts will be illustrated
by murals, statuary, dioramas, photos, maps, charts, documents, and
audio-visual displays.

The Statue of Liberty.

The story of immigration will unfold chronologically, with major emphasis on the period 1820–1920. During that time nearly 34 million recorded immigrants entered the United States.

The National Park Service hopes that Americans who visit the museum will leave with a glow of pride for the immigrants who braved the ocean to make a place for themselves in a strange new world.

MARINE MUSEUM OF THE SEAMEN'S CHURCH INSTITUTE
Address: 17 State St. (near Bowling Green), New York, N.Y.
Phone: BO 9-2710

Days: Daily 10–6. Saturday and Sunday 1–5. Closed Christmas and New Year's Day.
Admission: Free.

Subway: (1) IRT Lexington Ave. to Bowling Green station. (2) IRT 7th Ave. Change at Chambers St. for Lexington Ave. train.
Bus: Broadway bus to Bowling Green.
Auto: South on Broadway into State St. Metered street parking.

Restaurant: Basement cafeteria open to visitors to museum.

Gift Shop: Sales counter near 3rd-floor elevator has inexpensive publications on ships, small souvenirs, jewelry.

If you "must go down to the sea again, to the lonely sea and the sky," then the Marine Museum of the Seamen's Church Institute is the place for you. Here you will see whaling ships and clippers, freighters and junks, in a purposeful, panoramic view of the development of marine navigation and transportation for over two thousand years.

This museum is on the third floor of the Seamen's Church Institute, which began as a floating church in the East River. The institute has grown since 1843 from a floating chapel to the largest shore home in the world for merchant seamen. It is a self-contained community complete with a bank, clinic, and school; it also aids in locating missing seamen.

On top of the building is a lighthouse tower erected in 1913 as a memorial for the *Titanic*. Above the main doorway is a gilded figurehead of Sir Galahad. The ship's bell is from the *Atlantic,* which sank off Fishers Island in 1846.

The Marine Museum was founded in the middle 1950's, when gifts to the institute accumulated and were ultimately brought together as a special collection of ships' bells, paintings, anchors, memorabilia, and a vast number of ship models. | 19

The models are separated into four groups to show early development, native and work boats, steam and diesel boats, and picturesque and strange craft. There are models of an Egyptian barge (1850 B.C.), a Phoenician galley, gondola, Viking serpent ship, Tahitian outrigger

In the Marine Museum.

canoe, the *Half Moon* (Henry Hudson's ship), a Newfoundland fishing vessel, steamships, and a weird Korean "turtle" warship with armor plate. All the models are kept in humidity-controlled display cases. By means of its museum, the institute tells the fascinating story of the contributions to civilization made by men of the sea.

The museum archives and the Conrad Library on the same floor provide a file of general information on individual ships, as well as related information on oceanography, navigation, and nautical heraldry. The Marine Museum welcomes school groups.

In 1968 the museum will be installed in new quarters.

FRAUNCES TAVERN
Address: Corner of Broad and Pearl Sts., New York, N.Y.
Phone: (Sons of the Revolution) WH 4-6678

Days: Open weekdays, 10–4; Saturdays, 10–3. Closed Sundays and holidays (except Washington's Birthday), and Saturdays during July and August.
Admission: Free.

Subway: (1) IRT Lexington Ave. to Bowling Green station. (2) BMT Brighton (local) to Whitehall St.

Bus: Broadway bus to Pearl St. Walk east to Broad St.

Auto: South on Broadway into State St., left at Bridge St. to Broad St. Metered street parking.

Restaurant: Main floor of building is occupied by Fraunces Tavern Restaurant and Bar. Full-course meals.

Fraunces Tavern takes its name from Samuel Fraunces, a West Indian of French antecedents, who was the tavern's proprietor and a steward to George Washington. The first announcement advertising the establishment appeared in the New York *Gazette* of April 4, 1763: "At the Queens Head Tavern near the exchange or Long Bridge by Samuel Fraunces an ORDINARY dinner every day to be served at half after one."

The lower floors of the tavern now house a restaurant and bar. On the second floor is a "Long Room" with over thirty-five flags and banners. A bronze plaque says, "This room was the Scene of the Farewell of George Washington to his Officers on December 4, 1783." The scene is described by a Colonel Tallmadge in a diary owned by the Sons of the Revolution (not on display). Another plaque states, "This Shrine is Owned by and Maintained at the Expense of the Society of the Sons of the Revolution in the State of New York for the Benefit of the Public." (Not to be confused with the Sons of the American Revolution.)

The third floor displays a meaningless array of trivia in locked glass cases. Important-looking numbers label an old flintlock musket, pistols, water canteens, powder horns, epaulets, and an old shoe.

These items convey the spirit of the institution in which they are displayed. Fraunces Tavern, often billed as the oldest building in Manhattan, is, in fact, nothing more than a reconstruction of the famous tavern that once occupied this site. Since no view of the tavern has been found to exist earlier than one published in *Valentine's Manual* for 1853, the present building is an approximation of the original tavern's Georgian architecture.

Says Ada Louise Huxtable, architectural critic for *The New York Times:* "This landmark was built in 1907 virtually from scratch. It gives schoolchildren a fair idea of what a Georgian building looks like and gives local businessmen a fair lunch. But it is not old, it is not

Fraunces Tavern.

authentic and under no circumstances is this kind of thing preservation."

"Preservation," she points out, according to the National Trust for Historic Preservation, is the retention and repair of a genuine old building that still stands. "Restoration" is the more extensive work of putting a deteriorated landmark back in condition. "Reconstruction" is the erection of a modern copy of a no longer existing structure on the basis of educational value.

22 | 	Mrs. Huxtable continues, "It symbolizes a current attitude toward the architecture of the past so fallacious, so insidious, and so dangerous that those of us who have helped nurture the preservation movement in the country can do little more than weep."

Saddest of all, the mockery will increase, for the city plans to create "a unique living museum of outdoor architecture" on the Fraunces Tavern block, using the tavern as the nucleus. Architecture "of great historic importance" will be re-created from buildings in the Broad, Pearl, Water, Moore Streets and Coenties Slip area. To carry out this scheme, authentic buildings on the site will be torn down. Historic buildings that are moved here to take their place will become meaningless relics, with no relation to their original identity, site, and history. It is possible that this project may never materialize.

NEW YORK STOCK EXCHANGE EXHIBIT HALL

Address: 20 Broad St., New York, N.Y. (Additional visitors' entrance at 4 New St. is open during summer months.)
Phone: HA 2-4200, ext. 532

Days: Monday through Friday, 10–3:30.
Admission: Free.

Subway: IRT Lexington Ave. to Wall St. station.
Bus: Broadway bus to Wall St. East one block.
Auto: South on Broadway to Wall St. Limited meter parking.

Tours: Continuous guided tours available including film showing of 1 hour.

Special Restriction: Visitors may not go onto gallery carrying cameras or any objects that could be dropped over railing.

The New York Stock Exchange, in close proximity to Trinity Church and Federal Hall, was founded on May 17, 1792, after a group of merchants and auctioneers decided to meet regularly to buy and sell securities under an old buttonwood tree on Wall Street. In 1793, the twenty-four original members of the Exchange moved their operation indoors to the Tontine Coffee House. In succeeding years the Exchange occupied various quarters, until 1863, when it settled in its present location. The Exchange is now preparing to move again, this time about eight blocks south on Broad Street near Front Street, to a site recently cleared of its historic buildings. | 23

The present building, a landmark of sorts in the style known as Beaux Arts Eclectic, was designed by George B. Post and finished in 1903. Behind the six four-story Corinthian columns, an all-glass curtain wall provides light for the huge floor of the Exchange. The pediment sculpture group by John Quincy Adams Ward, when viewed from the street, looks like the downtrodden slaves of oppression, an incongruous choice for a building epitomizing American enterprise. The additional twenty-two stories of the Exchange hardly seem noticeable above this striking facade.

Every working day the main entrance on Broad Street sees a constantly moving crowd of stock clerks, tellers, office boys, secretaries, bankers, brokers, uniformed chauffeurs, and guards transporting securities in distinctive black valises on roller skates.

The Stock Exchange Exhibit Hall is on the third floor. The vivid story of capitalism is unfolded by means of documents, films, displays, ticker tape, and the Big Board. "Own a Share of American Business" exhorts an explanatory chart. Guided-tour lectures on what is a share of stock, how to read a stock table, and how an order is executed are presented by attractive hostesses. A number of interesting exhibits are by those who sell stock on the Exchange—Bristol Myers, Union Oil of California, Northern Natural Gas, I.B.M., and Avon products.

The New York Stock Exchange.

*Exhibit Hall in
the Stock Exchange.*

Kennecott Copper shows a miniature copper mine in operation. Children enjoy operating the machinery on display, pushing the various panel buttons, holding the earphones, watching slide films, and listening to the melodious voice of "Avon calling."

The long gallery that overlooks the entire Exchange floor affords a view of the workings of American enterprise in one of its most exciting phases.

FEDERAL HALL NATIONAL MEMORIAL
Address: Corner of Wall and Nassau Sts., New York, N.Y.
Phone: 264-4367

Days: Open Mondays to Fridays, 9–4:30, including all holidays.
Closed Thanksgiving, Christmas, and New Year's Day.
Admission: Free.

Subway: (1) BMT Brighton (local) to Fulton St. station. (2) IRT
Lexington Ave. to Wall St. station.
Bus: Broadway bus to Wall St. East one block.
Auto: South on Broadway to Wall St. Limited meter parking.

Tours: Guided tours available for groups; call in advance.

Federal Hall, with its great Doric columns and massive bronze statue of George Washington staring down Broad Street amid the newer buildings of metal and glass, still possesses a classic majesty.

Old City Hall was built in 1699. In 1765 the Stamp Act Congress met there; and in 1774, the first Continental Congress. The building was altered in 1788 and renamed Federal Hall before the first Congress under the Constitution convened. Washington took his presidential oath of office on the balcony on April 30, 1789. The Departments of State, War, and the Treasury were created, and the Bill of Rights was adopted on this site. In July, 1790, Washington, D.C. was chosen as the permanent capital of the nation, and by 1812 Federal Hall had been sold for salvage for $425.

The present Greek Revival structure was built in 1842 as a customs house. It was remodeled in 1862, and thereafter housed offices of the Subtreasury, Federal Reserve Bank, State Department, Passport Agency, Public Health Service, and other Federal departments until May, 1939, when it was designated a National Historic Site. Finally, on August 11, 1955, the building became a National Memorial administered by the National Park Service for "the inspiration and benefit of the people of the United States commemorating the founding of the Federal Government and related historic events."

The most significant object associated with Federal Hall is the Washington Stone in the rotunda room. It is a large rust-colored slab of sandstone (5' × 9½'), recovered from the balcony of the old Federal Hall, on which Washington stood while taking the oath of office. The Bible used in the inaugural ceremony is now owned by St. John's Masonic Lodge.

The Washington Room, up one flight, contains material pertaining to the first sixteen months of the Presidency—April 30, 1789, to August 30, 1790—in beautifully designed modern displays in well-illuminated cabinets. Miniature paintings, medals, snuffboxes, signed receipts, and bills of sale are in glass-covered pull-out drawers that contain the Messmore Kendall Collection of Washingtoniana. They were designed especially for the National Park Service.

The Bill of Rights Room is a gift from the American Bar Association. There is a translation from the Latin of the Magna Carta, and a diorama shows the debate over the Bill of Rights. Congress finally adopted twelve amendments on September 25, 1789, and sent them to the states for approval. Two were rejected, but the other ten became part of our Constitution on December 15, 1791. The copy originally sent to the state of Delaware is on display here.

Federal Hall.

The John Peter Zenger Room is dedicated to the journalist-printer who began his career as an apprentice to New York's first newspaper publisher (William Bradford, who is buried in Trinity churchyard). In 1733, Zenger founded his own *New York Weekly Journal.* After he exposed the corrupt administration of New York's Governor William Cosby, he was charged with seditious libel, imprisoned, and tried in the old City Hall building. Zenger's acquittal in 1735 was a landmark in the struggle for a free press in the Colonies.

CITY HALL GOVERNOR'S ROOM

Address: City Hall Park, Broadway and Park Row, New York, N.Y.
Phone: 566-5397

Days: Open daily, 10–3. Closed Saturdays, Sundays, and holidays.
Admission: Free.

Subway: (1) IRT Lexington Ave. to Brooklyn Bridge station. (2) BMT Brighton (local) to City Hall station.
Bus: Broadway bus to City Hall Park.
Auto: South on Broadway to Chambers St. Limited meter parking.

The Governor's Room in City Hall is a museum within a museum. The City Hall was designed by Joseph François Mangin and John McComb, Jr. McComb, who surpervised the job, was paid $6 a day, a considerable wage at that time. Construction was begun in 1803 and completed in 1812. A harmonious combination of French Renaissance and American Colonial influences, the building's two wings balance a central portico. Over the portico are the five arched windows of the Governor's Room.

The interior of City Hall is particularly fine. The first-floor rotunda is dominated by a superb double curving staircase with wrought-iron railings. The marble staircase leads to a ring of fluted Corinthian columns on the second floor. At the head of the stairs, on April 24th and 25th, 1865, the open bier of Abraham Lincoln was placed. Over 100,000 citizens climbed the winding staircase to view the martyred President.

The executive branch of the city's government occupies the first floor. The mayor's office is in the west wing, and the City Council president's is in the east wing. On the second floor the legislative arm is represented by the City Council in the east wing and the Board of Estimate in the west wing. The Board's public hearing room conveys the flavor of New York in the 1800's because of its white benches trimmed with dark mahogany. They are similar to the pews of the same period in historic St. Paul's Church.

The Governor's Room, on the second floor, is actually one large room with two small chambers on each side. It was originally set aside for use by the governor as a personal office when in the city. Long used for ceremonies, such as Lafayette's reception in 1824, it is now maintained as an important showcase for City Hall's antique furnishings and fine portraits of celebrated public officials associated with

| 29

Entrance to the Governor's Room in City Hall.

New York. Special conferences are still held in these chambers.

Recently, doubt was raised regarding the authenticity of the furnishings in the Governor's Room. The City Art Commission, after extensive research, uncovered documents, letters, and bills of sale that showed proof of their age and origin. The Washington Writing Table, chief cause of the controversy, was in use prior to 1790 at Federal Hall, the capital building of the new nation. The writing table, directly in the center of the Governor's Room, is considered the most notable object in the city's possession, and ranks with the foremost antique pieces in the country.

The John Trumbull portraits of George Washington (1790), George Clinton (1791), Alexander Hamilton, and John Jay (1805) were also originally installed in Federal Hall. Many of the exceptional portraits hang in various restricted areas of City Hall, but can be seen on application to the Art Commissioner's office.

Inside the Governor's Room.

FIRE DEPARTMENT MUSEUM

Address: 104 Duane St. (between Broadway and Church St.), New York, N.Y.

Phone: RH 4-1000. Ask for Engine 7, then for the museum.

Days: Open weekdays, 9–4; Saturdays, 9–1. Closed Sundays and all holidays.

Admission: Free.

Subway: (1) IND 8th Ave. to Chambers St. station. (2) BMT Brighton (local) to City Hall station. North 3 blocks.

Bus: Broadway bus to Duane St.

Auto: South on Broadway to Duane St. Limited meter parking.

Tours: For guided tours, obtain permission in advance from the Fire Commissioner, Municipal Building, New York 10007.

A famous 19th-century fire engine from New York City.

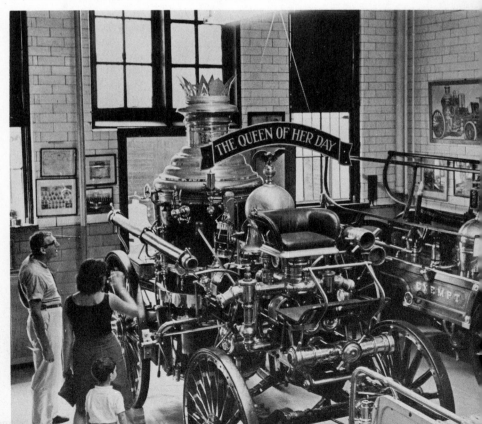

The Fire Department Museum occupies three floors of a building that would be an obvious choice for these collections—a firehouse. It is about three blocks north of City Hall. The museum, filled with engines, ladder trucks, tools, trophies, photographs, and documents, is a poignant memorial to the gallant and dedicated efforts of the New York City firemen, whose motto is "Prevent Fires! Save Lives!"

All the colorful, fascinating fire-fighting apparatus displayed was used in actual fire service during the nineteenth and early twentieth centuries. On the ground floor there are hand-drawn pumpers, horse-drawn and early motorized fire engines. A hand-drawn and hand-operated pumper, the Washington No. 1, built in 1820, has a leather hose with seams that are riveted together, a technique similar to that in the sewn hoses used in Holland as early as 1672.

A steam engine, the Silsby Steamer, in gleaming silver plate, was known as the queen of her day, and once pumped for thirty-nine hours continuously in a 1904 fire. There are also a La France steam engine with a pumping capacity of 700 gallons a minute, and a 1920 Model-T Ford for a deputy fire chief. One of the horse-drawn vehicles, built in 1853, is decorated with landscapes of Indian reservations and portraits of Indians in full headdress. The ground floor also has the first firebell, cast in England in 1796 and installed in a stone house that stood at Fulton and Front Streets. In the rear courtyard are alarm boxes, hose nozzles, gongs, and decorative stone sculpture portraits of firemen that appeared over early firehouse entrances.

The second floor has gooseneck hand pumpers, golden trumpets used by chiefs to issue orders, cases of medals, trophies, badges, uniforms, hatchets, fire helmets, and portraits of fire officials. There is also a section of the first water main constructed of wooden logs, laid in lower Manhattan in 1829.

In the center of the third floor is the Huguenot hose reel originally used in Staten Island. There are a number of torchlights, axes, firemen's diving hoods, and fireboat equipment. There is also a fire chief's sleigh, used until the turn of the century. A cut-away model of a firehouse shows the kitchen, bunks, brass sliding poles, and drying racks for hoses. The walls are hung with photographs of great fires which serve as a reminder that the purpose of the museum is to create public cooperation in fire prevention. | 33

Bright paint and brass
spangle another elaborate engine.

CHINATOWN MUSEUM
Address: 7 Mott St. (near Chatham Square), New York, N.Y.
Phone: WO 4-1542

Days: Open daily, 10–10.
Admission: Adults, $.50; children, $.25. Group rates available.

Subway: (1) BMT to Canal St. station. Walk two blocks east to Mott St. (2) IRT Lexington Ave. to Brooklyn Bridge station. North one block, east to Mott St.
Bus: Third Ave. bus to Mott St.
Auto: South on 3rd Ave. to Chatham Sq. Ample parking lots.

Gift Shop: Novelties and souvenirs.

Special Services: Tours and meals arranged for groups.

Lectures: Lecture tours for school groups recommended.

The Chinatown Museum is one of the busiest streets in New York's most exotic community, directly inside a penny arcade. The mixture of ancient Chinese culture in the museum and Pop-Art culture in the arcade has attracted thousands of school children, groups of Scouts, and visitors in the past five years.

When the museum was started by Herbert H. Weaver, his intention was to provide an educational facility for New York school children, whose field trips to Chinatown would be more meaningful if they had some idea about the Chinese—their cultural contributions, their history, theatre, music, religion, and even what and how they eat. The museum offers a tour of its exhibits, a tour of the Chinese community, and will even make luncheon and dinner arrangements for groups.

The museum has about ten exhibits that demonstrate Chinese culture clearly and simply. The main exhibit shows the course of Chinese history and what the Chinese have contributed to the progress of the world. All of the articles exhibited are still in use today, and instead of showing historic artifacts, the display contains such contemporary articles as modern playing cards, a dish of spaghetti, firecrackers, etc.

A display of ancient Chinese musical instruments incorporates a fascinating sight-and-sound device: the viewer pushes a button and then watches and hears a color film of the instrument being played. This unique technique offers a dramatic educational lesson.

Chinatown Museum.

One of the best exhibits reproduces the window of a Chinatown food store that has wax examples of every item that you can find in a typical Chinatown market. Over 200 Oriental foods are thus shown and identified.

The other exhibits show flowers and fruits and their symbolic meaning in Chinese culture, Chinese parade masks, the story of incense, of rice, etc. A Buddhist temple altar over 100 years old and a figure of Confucius are also included.

THE OLD MERCHANT'S HOUSE

Address: 29 East 4th St. (near the Bowery), New York, N.Y. | 35

Phone: SP 7-1089

Days: Open daily, 1–5; Sundays and holidays, 1–5. Closed Mondays, December 25, and the month of August. Phone in advance.

Admission: $.50. Special rates for public school classes.

Subway: IRT Lexington Ave. to Astor Place station. South to 4th St., then east 2 blocks.
Bus: Broadway or 3rd Ave. bus to 4th St.
Auto: Ample parking lots.

The street where the Old Merchant's House stands was once very fashionable, lined with beautiful town houses. Now there are trucking garages, factories, run-down lofts, and an occasional rooming house on the block.

The building is one of the finest examples of Classic Greek Revival architecture in the city. The only group of such town houses remaining intact stands along Washington Square North, a few blocks west. The Old Merchant's House is distinguished from the Washington Square buildings by its preservation of original furnishings and interiors, left exactly as they were in 1835 when Seabury Tredwell, a merchant and hardware importer, moved into the house, which had been built five years earlier by Joseph Brewster.

When Gertrude Tredwell, Seabury's last child, died in 1933, the Tredwell house and its contents were scheduled for public auction to satisfy debts and the mortgage. George Chapman, a distant relative, created the Historic Landmark Society to rescue the house. His purpose was to preserve it as a public museum displaying the family's entire belongings—paintings, furniture, china, lamps, books, even the framed diplomas from the fashionable girls' schools of the time.

In the house are trunks full of clothes, gowns, gloves, hats, Chantilly lace, paisley shawls, satin dancing slippers, even an exquisitely embroidered christening bonnet. Many of the trunks are not open, but may be seen on request.

With the exception of worn rugs and a number of broken cane chairs, most of the furniture and accessories are in good condition, particularly on the main floor, which is a huge double drawing room, cut in half with Corinthian columns and a sliding double door.

The principal bedrooms on the second floor have matching four-poster beds. All beds have canopies of silk and wool damask. The hall bedroom has a small pine tester bed with an arched chintz canopy. | 37 Although the surroundings seem elegant today, they were not considered luxurious a hundred years ago. Seabury Tredwell was an ultra-conservative person whose restrained good taste is evident throughout his house.

The Old Merchant's House.

In recent years the Old Merchant's House has visibly deteriorated. There are no funds available for repainting or for restoring walls and ceilings. The Federal Government recently designated the building as a national monument—which guarantees only the prestige conferred by a plaque and an official listing, but does not prevent any real-estate developer from destroying the building to acquire an apartment-house plot.

COOPER UNION MUSEUM FOR THE ARTS OF DECORATION

Address: Cooper Square at 7th St., New York, N.Y.
Phone: AL 4-6300

Days: Monday-Saturday 10–5. Closed on major holidays, and closed on Saturdays from June 1 to October 1.
Admission: Free.

Subway: (1) IRT Lexington Ave. to Astor Place station. (2) BMT Brighton (local) to 8th St. East 2 blocks.
Bus: Broadway, 3rd Ave., or 4th Ave. bus to Cooper Square.

Gift Shop: Sales counter near elevator offers pamphlets on topics related to arts of decoration.

The Cooper Union Museum for the Arts of Decoration is part of Cooper Union, a tuition-free college founded by a remarkable American engineer and philanthropist, Peter Cooper, a glue manufacturer, ironmaster, and locomotive builder who never had a formal education. The architect's study for Peter Cooper's "Museum of History, Art & Science" was prepared in 1853, but the official opening took place in May, 1897.

The building's Great Hall, on the first floor, was the scene of Abraham Lincoln's first public appearance in the East. Historians agree that this speech helped him win the presidential nomination.

The museum, which occupies the fourth floor, is rich in drawings, prints, wallpapers, furniture, and metalwork that represent a wide range of artistic creation of the past and present. The Textile-Design Collection, one of the finest in America, is primarily designed for research. Since all the collections and the textile study rooms are on one floor, the museum can be seen with relative ease. The fourth floor can be reached by a square elevator set in a cylindrical shaft that was provided for in the original plan of 1853, the same year Elisha Otis

| 39

Dining room and parlor.

first displayed his new steam-driven elevator at the Crystal Palace.
Flanking the elevator are two five-foot, elaborately decorated porcelain "oil jars with cover" from China, dated 1735–1759. In the first
exhibit hall an "Elements of Design" display depicts jugs, plants, draperies, and tankards showing *Surface* as a "textural character of an
object." Next comes *Form,* which "defines an object's shape in its
structural relation to space," and is illustrated with a sling chair by
Marcel Breuer, an earthenware charcoal stove, and a French cherry-
wood side chair. *Line,* or linear design, takes shape as a natural result
of the designer's use of particular materials, such as a wrought-iron
rocking chair, an ivory and wood birdcage, or a needle-lace panel.

Color presents the most fascinating and most difficult element of
design. There are color wheels and color charts, candelabra with cut
glass prisms reflecting color, a Tiffany vase with flowing strips of
color, and a fascinating light-color-box that has three rheostat knobs
which, when rotated, mix the primary colors together through a
filtered light source above. Since the color of light affects the surface

Cooper Union.
Exhibit based on "Form" in Cooper Union Museum.

it falls upon, another light box shows how a mixed-color abstract form is affected by the primary colors as each is switched on in turn.

Rhythm, as part of the "Elements of Design" display, is demonstrated by the orderly repetition of the designer's color, pattern, or motif, as in a carved oak panel with swirls and curlicues, or in a print that shows the repeated arches of a Gothic ceiling. In another gallery are examples of "Sources of Design," with illustrations.

The ceramics and glass collection includes creamware, black basalt, jasperware, Queen's ware, all manufactured by Wedgewood in England. There are cream pitchers, vegetable dishes, egg poachers, flowerpots, soup tureens, butter dishes, salters, and platters. The figurines of Meissen porcelain, with overglaze decoration of polychrome and gilt, are particularly handsome.

The textile collection and study rooms contain embroidery and prints on cotton, linen, and velvet dating from the third century, and showing designs from Turkey, Yemen, Egypt, India, Persia, China, Spain, and Italy. One embroidered twenty-one-inch panel from late sixteenth-century Italy shows adoring winged figures and winged cherubs' heads emerging from foliage, flower sprays, birds, fruits, and ribbons—all serving as an elaborate border around a small picture of the Nativity that is embroidered in pale silk and shaded in gold. Inside the circle are the kneeling Mary and Joseph, the Infant, shepherds, and angels. It is interesting how similar this panel is to religious greeting cards of the Victorian era.

In the Textile Gallery is an extraordinary English beadwork cabinet, the size of a lady's jewel box, with about eight tiny drawers. It was made in 1630. The most delicately miniscule colored-bead arrangements show the family coat of arms on the side doors and, on the top, a lady and her three attendants standing before a seated king.

In the same gallery are intricate examples of cuff flounces in needle lace from France, about 1690, showing flying figures, cupids, Indians, and fish cornucopias. These dramatic examples of elaborate laces, known as Points de France, were developed under the royal patronage of Louis XIV. From the sixteenth century until the Revolution, lace was worn as much by men as by women, as evidenced by their cravats, collars, and cuffs in portraits of this period.

42 | The Wallpaper Study Room contains superb, rare English, American, and French wallpaper designs, pilaster panels, overdoor panels, and borders. Some of the early examples are of leather tooled with fancy bird and flower designs. Above the wallpaper panels are seventy-five decorated Early American hatboxes.

Examples of antique furniture.

The large central gallery has small groupings of furniture; side chairs, sofas, small mahogany chests, secretaries, settees, sideboards, and satinwood writing tables. In a corner is a bass-fiddle-shaped Italian peepshow dated 1770. A large group of drawings in this gallery illustrates French and Italian theatrical designs from the mid-seventeenth century to about 1840.

In the last gallery, where floor-to-ceiling windows overlook Astor Place, are fascinating birdcages. One is shaped like a church, another a castle. One is an impressionistic replica of the Ponte Vecchio in Florence; still another is shaped like the cage of a circus animal. All are extremely delicate and intricately hand-constructed from thin tinplate. The wall opposite the cages displays pieces of pewter, brass, | 43 copper, decorated tinware, and some toleware. In the wrought-iron collection a bracket and lantern, together with a monumental balcony of diversified scrollwork from a bishop's palace, represent South German ironwork.

THEODORE ROOSEVELT BIRTHPLACE, N.H.S.

Address: 28 East 20th St. (between Broadway and 4th Ave.), New York, N.Y.
Phone: 573-6161

Days: Open daily, 9–4:30. Closed Thanksgiving, Christmas, and New Year's Day.
Admission: $.50. Children under 12 free. Special arrangements for group visits.

Subway: IRT Lexington Ave. to 23rd St. station, south to 20th St.
Bus: Madison Ave., 5th Ave., or Broadway bus to 20th St.
Auto: Limited meter parking.

Gift Shop: Commemorative medals, books on Theodore Roosevelt for sale.

A block west of Gramercy Park stands the massive five-story brownstone where Theodore Roosevelt, twenty-sixth President of the United States, was born and lived until he was fifteen years old. The only remaining brownstone on the street, its well-kept exterior is within steps of a "hero" sandwich shop, lofts, factories, a towel-supply company, and wholesalers of office equipment.

The Greek Revival house was built by Roosevelt's father. It is set back from the building line just enough to be almost unnoticeable from a distance. Only the American flag juts out, distinguishing the birthplace as a National Historic Site, under the supervision of the National Park Service of the Department of the Interior, with the cooperation of the Theodore Roosevelt Association, "to keep alive for future generations the life, the standards and the ideals of Theodore Roosevelt."

Five rooms and two museums are open to the public. The lower-floor museum presents a chronology of Roosevelt's life, from his birth on October 27, 1858, to his death on January 6, 1919. In about fifty desk-sized glass cases the display tells the story of the major events of Roosevelt's life: early childhood, college days to assemblyman, police commissioner, rancher, author, Assistant Secretary of the Navy, Rough Rider in the Cuban campaign of the Spanish-American War, Governor, President, hunter and explorer. The array of memorabilia is staggering: his personal diaries, bits of baby clothing, faded sepia family pictures and tintypes, zoological notebooks showing the animals captured and skinned, newspaper clippings highlighting significant events, political

44 |

Theodore Roosevelt's birthplace.

cartoons, sealskin caps, uniforms, bugles, mementos of the Inaugural Ball, relics of World War I, flowered teacups, and an elaborate selection of tin campaign buttons and emblems of miniature Rough Rider hats, whiskbrooms, eyeglasses, and elephants.

Roosevelt's accomplishments are highlighted in the Canal Zone commemorative postage stamps and the Nobel Peace Prize awarded him in 1906 for his efforts to end the Russo-Japanese War. A most unusual item on display is the book through which a bullet passed during an attempt to assassinate Roosevelt in 1912 in Milwaukee.

Roosevelt was born on the third floor. The bedroom, reached now by means of an elevator, is furnished in rosewood and satinwood. Next door, a charming nursery is set up with a little sleigh bed, dolls, and a child's tea set.

The furnishings on the elaborate parlor floor are the epitome of interior decoration in the Victorian era, "a period in which men of substance liked to have their homes reflect the dignity and solidity of their traditions and lives." These three rooms—parlor, library, and dining room—are furnished entirely in the style of that period, including the wallpaper, draperies, and carpets. In the library, the side chairs and sofa are upholstered in the expensive black horsehair that was so

The parlor.

46

fashionable in Victorian homes. Taken as a whole, this house-museum is a fascinating tribute to the colorful and important man born there.

POLICE ACADEMY MUSEUM
Address: 235 East 20th St. (near 2nd Ave.), New York, N.Y.
Phone: OR 7-1133

Days: Open weekdays, 9–5. Closed Saturdays, Sundays, and holidays.
Admission: Free.

Subway: IRT Lexington Ave. to 23rd St. station. South to 20th St.
Bus: 2nd Ave. or 3rd Ave. bus to 20th St.
Auto: Limited meter parking.

Tours: Two guided tours daily, at 10 and 2, cover Museum and Academy building. Groups must make appointment.

The purpose of the Police Academy Museum is to "inform the public, gain their support, emphasize the duties and obligations of the police, and to create a cooperative atmosphere between the police and the public."

New York City Patrolman Fred J. Levine, who is largely responsible for developing the concept of the museum, points out that the police must have public support and understanding in order to carry out their responsibilities: "It is true that Crime Does Not Pay, but only a small part of police work is devoted to chasing gangsters. The greatest percent is of a regulatory nature, that of being the protector of life and property, and the prevention of crime. In this museum we have developed a facility for people to come and learn the true role and function of the police."

The museum plays host to elementary-school children, teen-agers, adults, visiting law-enforcement officers, students of law and sociology, and it attempts to reach school dropouts, antisocial youths, and the underprivileged.

The exhibits cover gambling, counterfeiting, unlawful weapons, prostitution, suicide, homicide, historical memorabilia, and the training and recruitment of policemen. Two authoritative, outstanding exhibits illustrate the weapons used by youthful gangs and the narcotics racket.

Gang weapons, displayed in four glass cases, include machetes, meat cleavers, brass knuckles, ice picks, and an assortment of homemade zip guns. The narcotics display includes the plants from which

A "tommy gun" hidden in a violin case.

drugs are obtained, and all the paraphernalia used by addicts: needles, syringes, rubber bands, bent spoons, pipes, and so on.

In addition to the museum on the second floor of the new building of the Police Academy, visitors are encouraged to tour the entire building, where they are shown the work of the ballistics and bomb squads, the police-evidence laboratory, emergency service division, gymnasium, and the firing range where demonstrations are given.

BOXING HALL OF FAME
Address: 120 West 31st St. (between 6th and 7th Aves.), New York, N.Y.

Phone: 564-0354

Days: Open weekdays, 10–4. Closed Saturdays, Sundays, and holidays.
Admission: Free.

Various displays in the Police Museum.

Subway: (1) IND 6th Ave. to 34th St. station. (2) IRT 7th Ave. to 34th St. station. South 3 blocks.
Bus: 6th Ave. or 7th Ave. bus to 31st St.
Auto: No parking available.

Perhaps the most offbeat museum in New York is the Boxing Museum, located in an old loft building on the edge of the garment district. The principle attraction here is fist sculpture, arranged row on row in showcases in the reception room of *The Ring* magazine. The museum also displays collections of fighters' photographs, gongs, timers, pocket watches donated by famous boxers and sportsmen, a wide array of boxing gloves, punching bags, and championship belts.

The fist sculpture, created by Dr. Walter H. Jacobs, a dentist, shows in fifty bronze-colored plaster casts the huge fist of Primo Carnera, the deadly fist of Joe Louis, and the fists of Rocky Graziano, Jack Johnson, Floyd Patterson, and others. Another memento is a typed letter addressed to the magazine's editor, Nat Fleischer, dated

Casts of famous boxers' fists.

Paris, January 27, 1916, in which Jack Johnson confesses he faked the fight with Jess Willard. Mr. Fleischer, who saw the contest, says it was legitimate. He claims Johnson spun the yarn in order to make some money on the story.

As there are no other archives of this type, it can be said that this collection of memorabilia has real historical value for boxing buffs.

THE PIERPONT MORGAN LIBRARY

Address: 29 East 36th St. (at Madison Ave.), New York, N.Y.
Phone: MU 5-0008

Days: Open daily, 9:30–5. Exhibition area closed Saturdays in June and July, Sundays, legal holidays, and the month of August.
Admission: Free.

Subway: IRT Lexington Ave. to 33rd St. station. North to 36th St., then west.
Bus: Fifth or Madison Ave. bus to 36th St.
Auto: Limited garage parking.

Special restrictions: No cameras allowed.

The Pierpont Morgan Library serves as a reminder of the Victorian era when Murray Hill was a fashionable residential section containing, in the last decades of the nineteenth century, dwellings of many of New York's Four Hundred—the Belmonts, Rhinelanders, Tiffanys, Havemeyers, and its leading citizen, J. Pierpont Morgan, financier and collector.

Morgan began collecting from the time he went abroad to school in 1854. Wealthy and educated, he felt no need to rely on the taste or judgment of art experts. He bought what he liked. Morgan believed the surest way to learn about art was to keep looking at it. His father, Junius Morgan, had also been a collector. He owned a six-page letter, written by George Washington in 1788 expressing his hopes for the new nation. The letter is in the library today.

It was not until 1890, when Junius Morgan was killed in a carriage accident on the Riviera, that Pierpont Morgan began to collect in earnest, and on a grand scale. He bought a copy of the Gutenberg Bible on vellum, four Shakespeare folios, and manuscripts by Keats, Dickens, and Byron, to name a few. Eventually he began to accumulate whole libraries of other collectors. In ten years his collection assumed monumental proportions. At that point he commissioned the architectural firm of McKim, Mead and White to provide a beautiful setting for his treasured manuscripts and works of art. Charles F. McKim under- | 51 took the assignment himself, and in 1906 finished the Renaissance palazzo built in the classic Greek manner of fitted marble blocks. The building has become one of New York's classic landmarks.

By the time of Morgan's death, in 1913, his library was renowned

The Pierpont Morgan Library.

as the finest private collection in the United States. In his will, Morgan said, "It has been my desire and intention to make some suitable disposition of my collections which would render them permanently available for the instruction and pleasure of the American people." His son continued the collections with the assistance of Miss Belle Da Costa Greene, library director for forty-three years. In 1924, believing that the library had achieved too important a position to remain in private hands, J. P. Morgan transferred it to a board of trustees, with an endowment to provide for maintenance. It was incorporated as a public reference library.

In the mansion around the corner, at Madison and 37th, Pierpont's son, J. P. Morgan lived. The landmark is apparently now slated for demolition. In 1945, two years after J. P. Morgan died, the Lutheran Church in America bought the building for $245,000, and now, because of cramped quarters, it may build a twenty-one-story office tower on the site. The old mansion is a forty-five-room Victorian brownstone, built in the 1840's, in Renaissance revival style, with graceful balconies and wrought-iron grillwork. It is separated from the library by a small garden.

The main entrance to the Morgan Library is through the Annex, at the corner of Madison and 36th Street. This was originally the site of Pierpont's house. A scholars' reading room, on the right, is open for study and research by accredited students and research workers. The library issues a four-page folder of stringent rules pertaining to the use of its material.

The only manuscripts that can be seen by the general public are those on exhibition, under glass, to the left of the reading room. Except for periods during the summer, there are frequent exhibitions of varying duration. The long corridor that leads to the two principal galleries contains a print exhibition, a section devoted to French bindings, and a literature sales desk.

In the West Room, the study, Pierpont Morgan was host to royalty, politicians, ecclesiastical figures, foreign dignitaries, art dealers, collectors, scholars, intellectuals, writers, and the group of bankers whom Morgan assembled there to stem the financial panic of 1907. The walls are hung with a silk damask of intense red that provides a magnificent background for the paintings, sculpture, massive furniture, stained-glass windows, marble mantelpiece, and decorated ceiling. A handsome marble vestibule separates the West Room from the East Room. | 53

The East Room is stacked from floor to ceiling with three tiers of bookcases. A huge tapestry hangs over a monumental marble fireplace, and stairs used to reach the two upper tiers of books appear when the bookcases nearest the doors are half turned, like a revolving door. A modern electronic fire-detection system and an atmospheric control system protect some of the greatest literary treasures in the Western Hemisphere.

The library is outstanding in the fields of English, American, French, and Italian autograph manuscripts and medieval and Renaissance manuscripts from the sixth to the sixteenth centuries. The books date from the inception of printing, and include some from the press of the first English printer, William Caxton. There is also a collection of etchings by Rembrandt.

The library maintains an active acquisition program. Its most recent achievement was the purchase of a section of the Book of Hours made for Catherine of Cleves. These books of the 14th and 15th centuries were commissioned by individuals for their private devotions and were profusely illuminated with miniatures. For over a hundred years it was believed that this Book of Hours, belonging to the Guennol Collection on Long Island, was complete. Then Frederick B. Adams, Jr., director of the library, found that another part existed. Both parts of the book were put on display at the library in 1964. With its 157 dazzling miniatures, it is the finest Dutch manuscript in existence.

THE NEW YORK PUBLIC LIBRARY

Address: Fifth Ave. at 42nd St., New York, N.Y.
Phone: OX 5-4200

Days: Open weekdays, 9–10; Sundays and holidays, 1–10. Exhibition room (318) open Monday-Saturday, 9–5.
Admission: Free.

Subway: (1) IND 6th Ave. to 42nd St. station, then east. (2) IRT Lexington Ave. to 42nd St. station, then west.
Bus: Fifth Ave. or Madison Ave. bus to 42nd St.
Auto: No parking available.

54 | *Gift Shop:* Publications sales desk in main lobby.

It is difficult to imagine the time when anything else was on the site where the New York Public Library now stands. But before this monumental library was built in 1911—taking fourteen years—the enorm-

The New York Public Library.

ous, high-walled brick basin of the Croton Reservoir stood on the corner of what is now one of the busiest intersections in the United States. The library, designed by Carrere & Hastings, is deeply set back from Fifth Avenue, ornamented with Corinthian columns, sculpture, water fountains, urns, and the two famous library lions, of the species that appears in civic architecture from Trafalgar Square to Baltimore to Fifth Avenue.

The New York Public Library is second in size in America only to the Library of Congress. The entire system consists of eighty community branches, four mobile units, and the main reference building on Fifth Avenue. The library is a result of the consolidation of three private libraries founded separately by John Jacob Astor, James Lenox, and Samuel Jones Tilden. These original libraries constitute the Reference Collection, largely supported today by private funds. The daily attendance is over 8,500.

Among its invaluable holdings are the handwritten copy of Washington's Farewell Address, the first Gutenberg Bible brought to America, Jefferson's early draft of the Declaration of Independence, the Dongan Charter of New York City, dated 1686; and a copy of the New York *Gazette* dated 1726, the first newspaper published in New York. The library itself regularly publishes bibliographies, facsimiles, and material concerning literary research.

The library has an invaluable collection of pamphlets, many of which are the only ones in existence. The same is true for its countless periodicals, journals, broadsides, scrapbooks, song sheets, and other documents.

A logical starting point to see the exhibits is the entrance hall at the top of the stairs at the Fifth Avenue entrance. In the enormous lobby are a series of display cases in which a wide variety of books are regularly exhibited. "The Bible and Its Illustrators," "Illustrations from Dante," "Gaelic Books," "Music of the Shakers," and "Images of America" are titles of exhibitions in recent years.

A comprehensive explanation of the development of printing is displayed along the left corridor. At the right side of the lobby a new sales shop carries a wide range of publications pertaining to book research, techniques, and the art of printing and letters. The Miller Collection of United States postage stamps (1850–1901) is set in the wall to the right of the information desk. From here you can take the elevator to the third floor.

Halls on the third floor are lined with Currier & Ives prints of the "Life of the Fireman" and colored stone engravings of a number of American cities. These early views are from the Phelps Stokes Collection.

The Exhibition Room (318) is open to the public. It offers changing displays of manuscripts, mainly from the Berg Collection of English and American literature. Original manuscripts are often illegible and bear numerous corrections, but they are of special interest to students and scholars who may see here manuscripts by many famous authors.

Paintings by John Trumbull, Gilbert Stuart, and Joshua Reynolds are in the library's collection. In the central hall hangs a classic example of the Hudson River School of painting by Asher Brown Durant, who depicted two of his friends, William Cullen Bryant and Thomas Cole, standing on a rocky ledge overlooking a peaceful gorge.

Entrance hall of the library.

In the south corridor are the Print Gallery, the Print Room (308), and Art and Architecture (313), which are open to the public. Some of the other rooms, the Berg Collection (320), Arents Collection (324), Manuscripts (319), and Rare Books (303), require a special admission card from the director's office. But for the most part, the general visitor strolling through the building would be sufficiently occupied by the rooms and resources open to the public.

The Central Card Catalogue (315) has 10 million file cards, in 10,000 card trays, that cover every imaginable subject. After a specific book title has been found in the card files and a call slip filed, the book may be picked up by the reader in either one of the huge main reading rooms. They are two blocks long, and can seat 700 readers. The entire Theatre Collection, which was just off the Main North Reading Room, was recently removed to Lincoln Center. Still near the main reading rooms are the genealogy and history rooms.

The second floor occasionally has an exhibition relating to New York history, with maps, manuscripts, and documents. It also houses the Jewish, Slavonic, and Oriental Literature departments and the Economics and Sociology divisions. The first floor, in addition to exhibitions, houses Science and Technology departments and Periodicals and Maps. The Central Circulation Library, Picture Collection, and Children's Room are downstairs on the ground floor. There is a convenient entrance on the 42nd-Street side of the library.

Perhaps the best way to describe the value of the New York Public Library is to quote from one of its own booklets, written by William K. Zinsser: "The quality that makes the Library great is one that runs deeper than men and books. It is the quality of freedom. This is a building that takes no sides because it presents all sides. It grants its visitors the dignity of free access to information . . . [and] operates on the belief that free men will find the truth."

ALLIED CHEMICAL EXHIBITION CENTER
Address: 1 Times Square, New York, N.Y.
Phone: HA 2-7300, ext. 491.

Days: Open Tuesdays to Saturdays, 11–8.
Admission: Free.

Subway: BMT, IND 8th and 6th Ave., IRT 7th Ave. subways to Times Square station.
Bus: Broadway or 7th Ave. bus to Times Square.
Auto: No parking available.

Fashion on parade
in the Allied Chemical
Exhibition Center.

Events: Magic show; fashion show 5 times daily.

Once a distinguished New York landmark, *The New York Times* Tower in Times Square has recently been transformed into a gleaming, cream-colored, windowless, hard-edge modern building that is the headquarters for the Allied Chemical Corporation. On the first three floors an exhibit center displays the company's participation in moon exploration, its research in chemistry, agriculture, shelter, and recreation, and its success in creating new products and materials.

The first floor features an animated demonstration of the moon landing planned for the Apollo Space Project and an animated diorama of an imaginary city on the moon called Copernicus as it might appear in the year 2000. In the moon-city model one can see a construction project, lunar surface vehicles, space laboratories, and weather stations. | 59

On the second floor there are displays of basic chemical processes. One interesting cross-section model shows the composition of the earth's substrata. Small discs and pointers indicate the greatest depths at which the planet's sixteen principal elements are found. One of the best exhibits demonstrates how modern chemistry has taken the basic elements and transformed them into materials stronger than steel, softer than feathers, more flexible than rubber, and more durable than varnish.

The visitor should not miss the fashion show on the third floor, which features the many uses of Caprolan Nylon made by Allied Chemical.

UNION CARBIDE EXHIBIT HALL

Address: 270 Park Ave. (between 47th and 48th Sts.), New York, N.Y.
Phone: 551-2345

Days: Open weekdays, 9–6; Saturdays, 10–5. Closed Sundays and holidays.
Admission: Free.

Subway: IRT Lexington Ave. to 51st St. station. Walk west to Park Ave., south to building.
Bus: Fifth or Madison Ave. bus to 48th St.
Auto: Limited garage parking.

Some of the jet-age business buildings on Park Avenue have put their best space forward for the purpose of exhibitions, some permanent, some temporary. The Lever Building, at 53rd Street, gives its street-floor space to art exhibits. The Pepsi-Cola Company has presented delightful children's shows at Christmastime. But the company whose offerings have not been duplicated by local galleries or museums is Union Carbide, the second largest chemical company in the world.

Its first contribution, "Atomic Energy in Action," was on exhibit for five years. An educational display lasting that long has to be good. The exhibit was a unique blend of architecture, electronics, and art designed by Will Burtin, an expert on three-dimensional and industrial designs. It told the story of uranium, beginning with man's concept of the atom in 500 B.C. It presented the world's largest operating model of a uranium-235 atom, a large-scale operating model of a pool-type research reactor; a 60-foot-long animated mural of a nuclear chain reaction; and a display showing how uranium is mined, milled, and used in reactors. The exhibit was designed to give the public a better understanding of the peaceful uses of atomic energy. The dismantled exhibit will probably be donated to the University of California.

The next phase of the company's exhibition program will stress the

Scientific exhibit in Union Carbide Exhibit Hall.

theme of peace through understanding and international cooperation, with the installation of major exhibitions expressing the modern cultures of foreign countries. A major event on the agenda is the Japan Art Festival. A photography and memorabilia show of people, places, and things will be based on a National Geographic Society expedition.

Rotating exhibits of lesser dimension are held in the street-floor lobby "galleries" at the foot of the escalators, but the principal exhibit is presented in the block-long space on the second floor. This is actually one huge room, two stories high, divided into two sections by the tower core of the fifty-two-story structure.

The Union Carbide building was designed by Skidmore, Owings and Merrill. In the lobby a curved directory board and an electronic control panel show the location and direction of movement of all the elevators in the building. It is a work of art. The black porcelain enamel-textured stainless-steel column-covers and the fluted stainless-steel curtain walls make a truly dramatic, optically invigorating, gleaming interior.

| 61

CHASE MANHATTAN BANK MONEY MUSEUM
Address: 1254 Ave. of the Americas (6th Ave.) at 50th St., New York, N.Y.
Phone: 552-1046, Ext. 248

Days: Open Tuesdays through Saturdays, 10–5. Closed holidays.
Admission: Free.

Subway: IND 6th Ave. to 49th St. station.
Bus: 5th Ave. or 6th Ave. bus to 50th St.
Auto: Limited garage parking.

Tours: No guided tours, but student groups, clubs, and organizations should call in advance of arrival.

The Chase Manhattan Bank Money Museum is at street level in the R.C.A. building, situated near the Time/Life building, Radio City Music Hall, and Whelan's drugstore, on one of the busiest corners in New York. Its location obviously helps to put a grand total on the attendance meter. But a museum featuring money would probably have little attendance trouble no matter where it was located.

The money museum is the largest museum of this type in the United States, and reveals in these exhibits that "money is a study of man's history, art, social customs and religious beliefs." The 75,000 historical, curious, exotic, and valuable items are protected by two guards, one for each gallery. One gallery has money from foreign countries; the other contains United States coins, notes, and documents, including a $100,000 gold certificate recently acquired.

The monies are mounted in alcove groupings that detail the story of money by means of ancient coins, primitive money, United States and foreign coins, counterfeits, and paper money. A block of unusual checks shows that each one has been endorsed by a President of the United States.

Primitive money has been made of many useful, scarce, or valuable commodities. Tree money, for instance, is a product of the more sophisticated societies in China, Japan, and Malaya. Metal coins, cast in tree-shaped molds, were broken off at the stem when needed.

The first wooden nickels can be seen among a large assortment of "emergency" money—that is, notes and scrip issued during panics, money shortages, depressions, and printed on sheepskin, fishskin, leather, wood, or clamshells. Tigers' tongues, elephants' tails, bronze bells, wampum, and tobacco have also been used as money.

62 |

One oddity on display is a check of the Lincoln Electric Co. canceled by submachine-gun bullets. This improbable check was made out, signed, and endorsed by arc-welding on a section of one-eighth-inch steel plate (12 inches by 24 inches). It was canceled by a Cleve-

Exhibits in the Chase Money Museum.

land Trust Company bank teller who wrote PAID with a shower of bullets. Another eyecatching exhibit contains Confederate and counterfeit money and amusing nineteenth-century American cast-iron "piggy" banks that swallowed coins.

If one leaves the museum with any doubt about the purpose of the Chase Manhattan Bank, it is best dispelled in the final line of its souvenir booklet: ". . . our chief concern about money is only how to acquire more of it."

TIME/LIFE EXHIBITION CENTER
Address: Time/Life Building, Ave. of the Americas (6th Ave.) at 50th St., New York, N.Y.
Phone: JU 6-1212

Days: Open weekdays, 9–5. Saturdays, Sundays, and holidays, 11–7; exhibitions as announced.
Admission: Free.

Subway: IND 6th Ave. to 49th St. station.
Bus: 5th Ave. or 6th Ave. bus to 50th St.
Auto: Limited garage parking.

Gift Shop: Subscriptions to Time, Inc. magazines and hard-cover publications on sale at counter. Small souvenirs also available.

Exhibits on art, photography, science, history, and politics have brought nearly 3 million people to the Time/Life Exhibition Center since it opened in January, 1961, with "Since Time Began," a show that highlighted important world events since the first issue of *Time* magazine was published in 1923.

The purpose of the Exhibition Center is outlined by Time President James A. Linen: "Through our exhibits we believe we are adding an extra dimension to our communication effort and making a further contribution to the understanding and appreciation of beauty and art as well as news. . . . We search for something that is interesting, dramatic and timely; something which is not elsewhere available to the public. We look first for artistic merit and if the exhibit can logically reflect the journalistic achievements of our company, that is an additional value."

The Exhibition Center is a hundred-foot hall with a two-story glass front that forms a backdrop to the popular fountains on 6th Avenue. The hall's thirty-two-foot-high ceiling is studded with aluminum and plastic disks of different sizes, suspended at varying distances from one another. Some of the disks move with the air currents. The ceiling was designed by Wallace K. Harrison.

64 | On the second level, across the west and north walls runs a balcony used for exhibits and a widely stocked reference library of United States and European magazines and newspapers, standard reference works, and a complete file of Time, Inc. publications. This mezzanine library is open to the public, and a trained librarian is in attendance.

Time/Life
Exhibition Center.

MUSEUM OF FAMOUS PEOPLE

Address: 133 West 50th St. (between 6th and 7th Aves.), New York,
N.Y.

Phone: JU 6-2616

Days: Open daily: Mondays to Thursdays, 10–8:30; Fridays, 10–10:30;
Saturdays, 10–11:30; Sundays, 12–10:30.

Admission: Adults, $1.25; children, $.60. Group rates available.

"The Roaring '20's"
wax display in the
Museum of Famous People.

Subway: (1) IND 6th Ave. to 49th St. station. (2) IND 8th Ave. to 7th Ave. station.

Bus: 6th Ave. or 7th Ave. bus to 50th St.

Auto: Limited garage parking.

Gift Shop: Novelties and souvenirs on sale.

66 | Bringing London's Madame Tussaud's Wax Museum up to date, the Museum of Famous People has molded its characters in plastic. Unlike the traditional wax figures that have a tendency to melt, these 160 life-size vinyl-plastic reproductions are a "dramatic advance over traditional wax museums." To the average person, however, these plastic figures are indistinguishable from those made of wax at Ripley's Paris Wax Museum, 1539 Broadway.

This new museum is a great deal larger than that on Broadway. It covers about half an acre of underground passageways containing about fifty "son et lumière" (sound and light) tableaus and dioramas depicting famous people and incidents in history. This fascinating method of presentation greatly enhances the historic significance of the person shown for both children and adults.

Thus the visitor will find Aaron Burr and Alexander Hamilton in a realistic staging of their famous duel—complete with birds chirping overhead and crickets down below; a dramatic scene of the tragic Triangle Shirtwaist fire in lower Manhattan; a scene from the famous Stage Door Canteen of World War II; Harry Houdini escaping from an underwater box; and the Kennedy family in mourning, including John, Jr. saluting. The figures in the gallery include many notables in contemporary life—from singing stars to astronauts.

MUSEUM OF AMERICAN FOLK ART
Address: 49 West 53rd St. (near 6th Ave.), New York, N.Y.
Phone: LT 1-2474

Days: Open daily, except Mondays, 10:30–5:30.
Admission: $.25.

Subway: IND 8th Ave. "E" train or 6th Ave. "F" train to Fifth Ave. station (53rd St.).
Bus: 5th Ave. or 6th Ave. bus to 53rd St.
Auto: Limited garage parking.

Membership: Annual membership $15.00 up. Benefits include admission to all exhibitions for two persons, newsletters, invitations to special lectures and films.

The Museum of American Folk Art was opened in 1963. It is the first museum in New York City devoted exclusively to the exhibition and study of the work of untutored native artist-craftsmen. The fascination of folk art and its universal appeal to housewives, children, collectors, businessmen, artists, designers, and teen-agers have already established this museum as a permanent and useful member of the art | 67 community.

Aside from providing entertainment and education, the museum has another purpose: "To display and collect the arts which embody the creative individuality of our people and to offer an historical back-

ground for the contemporary American scene." The museum acts also as a clearinghouse for research and information on folk artists, known by name or by style, and eventually hopes to establish a folk-art index of photographs, slides, and manuscripts documenting the works of American folk artists.

The museum occupies one floor of a spacious studio building on the same street as the Museum of Modern Art and the Museum of Contemporary Crafts. Although its quarters, by comparison with other museums, could be considered small, the quality and depth of its exhibitions more than compensate. In its short lifespan the museum has offered impressive exhibitions. "Turning in the Wind" displayed rare and unusual nineteenth-century weathervanes, hand-carved weather devices, and wind toys in such forms as angels, butterflies, chickens, soldiers on horseback, all painstakingly carved and sensitively colored. These objects showed the strength and individuality of the folk tradition in American art and design.

Other exhibits have been "Rubbings from New England Gravestones," one of the oldest forms of folk art; "The Art of the Decoy"; "The American Image," paintings and sculpture featuring American symbols and Presidents; the paintings of Erastus Salisbury Field, one of the most famous of nineteenth-century American folk artists; "Religion in Wood: A Study in Shaker Design"—an outstanding collection of Shaker furnishings; and "Santos: The Religious Folk Art of New Mexico," in which carved figures and painted panels expressed in naïve, colorful terms the splendor and horror of Christ's Passion, together with figures of Spanish saints.

From its members and from private donors the museum is gradually accumulating its own permanent collection. Notable acquisitions have been two limestone sculptures by Will Edmondson, a Nashville folk carver; a wooden gate of c. 1872 made to look like a contemporary American flag; a huge yellow weathervane in the form of an Indian chief and called "Chief Tammany"; a carved and painted eagle made about 1900 by Bernier of Maine, some decoys, Sunday-school samplers, and early tin toys.

As the museum grows its programs expand. Five new shows, historic village and house tours, lectures and movies, and folk-art tours of Central Europe are part of its future plans. | 69

The angel Gabriel blows his horn
in the Museum of American Folk Art.

A whirligig and an example of Pennsylvania Dutch painting.

The museum is dependent on individual gifts and memberships for operating funds. As the director, Mary Childs Black, wrote in her quarterly newsletter: "Not only do we need membership support to strengthen our interests and programs in Manhattan, but, plainly, we need financial aid from those most interested in helping the Museum to succeed."

This "Punch" was a 19th-century cigar store figure.

MUSEUM OF CONTEMPORARY CRAFTS

Address: 29 West 53rd St. (between 5th and 6th Aves.), New York, N.Y.
Phone: CI 6-6840

Days: Open Mondays through Saturdays, 11–6; Sundays, 1–6. Library open Mondays through Fridays, 10–5.
Admission: Free.

Subway: IND 8th Ave. "E" train or 6th Ave. "F" train to Fifth Ave. station (53rd St.).
Bus: 5th Ave. or 6th Ave. bus to 53rd St.
Auto: Limited garage parking.

Membership: Subscribing and craftsman membership, $8.00 and $12.00 and up. Privileges include subscription to *Craft Horizons* magazine, previews, etc.

The Museum of Contemporary Crafts has gradually elevated public consciousness of crafts as a true form of artistic expression. Its presentations offer living craft art, changing exhibitions of ceramics, woven and printed textiles, metalwork, enameling, and fibers. The museum also encourages and stimulates working artists, and has shown the works of thousands of craftsmen during the past ten years, since it was opened by its parent organization, the American Craftsmen's Council.

The museum offers about five shows a year, which have attracted some 110,000 visitors annually. Their variety is indicated by their titles: "Stage Design Models," "Louis Comfort Tiffany," "World of Puppets," "1000 Years of Pottery in America," "Contemporary French Bookbinding," "Glass: Czechoslovakia and Italy," and "The Art of Personal Adornment."

Much of the success of recent exhibitions can be attributed to the dynamic and inspiring leadership of Paul J. Smith, Director. One of the recent shows that drew a record attendance (44,000) was entitled "Amusements." A collection of objects and games focused attention on the experience of fun and play for adults as well as children.

72 |

Usually there are three exhibitions held at once, a group show, a one-man show, and a survey show with a special theme. The main gallery on the first floor and second level is used for the leading exhibit. The Little Gallery, a large alcove on the second floor, is set aside for

Modern interpretations of classic forms in porcelain.

*New forms in ceramics from California
at the Museum of Contemporary Crafts.*

showing the work of one craftsman. The third-floor Members Gallery, formerly the restaurant, is also used to display the crafts of a single artist. The front half of this floor is used for the Service and Information Center of the museum and the Craftsmen's Council. The council's offices are on the fourth floor.

The council is a nonprofit national membership organization chartered by the Board of Regents of New York. It was founded in 1943 by Mrs. Vanderbilt Webb, and opened the museum in 1956. Primarily, the council acts as an educational and professional service organization "to promote every aspect of craftsmanship and the use of craft products for the enrichment of our lives and culture." It receives no government support other than tax exemption.

Although there is nothing for sale in the museum, crafts can be purchased through its affiliate, America House, across the street. The council also keeps up-to-date files on active craftsmen, and examples of their work. These files, on the fourth floor, are open to the public. An architect's service assists in locating craftsmen to collaborate on projects. There are also a catalogue and file on craft schools. Another council service is a Portable Museum, consisting of slide kits, films, and other visual aids about crafts and craftsmen. These kits may be rented.

The council also sponsors lectures and conferences. It is responsible for the formation of the World Crafts Council, an international organization for facilitating communications in the world of crafts; and it founded the School of American Craftsmen at the Rochester Institute of Technology. It is the publisher of *Craft Horizons*. There is also a Museum West of the American Craftsmen's Council in San Francisco.

THE MUSEUM OF MODERN ART
Address: 11 West 53rd St. (near 5th Ave.), New York, N.Y.
Phone: CI 5-8900

Days: Monday through Saturday, 11–6; Thursdays till 9, Sundays, 12 noon to 6. Closed Christmas Day.
Admission: Adults $1.25, children under 16, $.50. Special group rates by advance arrangement with Information Center.

Subway: IND 8th Ave. "E" train or 6th Ave. "F" train to 5th Ave. station (53rd St.).
Bus: 5th Ave. or 6th Ave. bus to 53rd St.
Auto: Limited garage parking.

Restaurant: Garden restaurant has complete luncheons, tea, and dinner on Thursday only. Members' restaurant in Penthouse.

Gift shop: Museum shop in lobby is well stocked with books, catalogues, reproductions, stationery.

Special Events: Film showings, 2 and 5:30 daily. Thursday at 8, Saturday at 11:30, 3:00, and 5:30. Art classes for children, young people, and adults. Art lending service, concerts, symposiums, lectures, as announced.

Membership (annual): $22.00, New York area residents; $18.00, non-residents. Benefits include free admission to museum for husband and wife, invitations to previews, exclusive use of Penthouse restaurant, free publications, etc.

Tours: Gallery talks as announced in the monthly Calendar of Events.

In the sculpture garden.

"Guernica" by Pablo Picasso.

At the Museum of Modern Art trends are launched, tastes formed, and the social scene is set. The museum is the place to see a Picasso, have lunch in the Sculpture Garden, listen to a lecture, watch an old film, steep yourself in jazz, drink champagne at an opening, meet your wife or friends, take your children, and, of course, see the *avant-garde* art of Europe and America. As a great contemporary force, the museum has made its mark on America by raising popular aesthetic standards to a new level.

The Museum of Modern Art was the product of three pioneering collectors: Abby Aldrich Rockefeller, wife of John D. Rockefeller, Jr.; Lillie P. Bliss, and Mrs. Cornelius J. Sullivan. They were joined by A. Conger Goodyear, Frank Crowninshield, Mrs. Murray Crane, Dr. Paul J. Sachs, Stephen C. Clark, Chester Dale, Duncan Phillips, and Sam Lewisohn in forming the museum. In July, 1929, the Regents of the University of the State of New York granted a charter for | 77 "establishing and maintaining a museum of modern art, encouraging and developing the study of modern arts and furnishing popular instruction." The founders intended to establish a collection of the immediate ancestors of the modern movement and the most important living masters. Forming a collection of contemporary art was in itself a gamble, but to attempt to establish a museum of modern art was a daring commitment during the beginning and worst years of the Great Depression.

Alfred H. Barr, Jr., who was then twenty-seven, was appointed director of the museum. The first exhibition opened on November 7, 1929, in the Heckscher Building at 730 Fifth Avenue.

This landmark exhibition contained 35 Cézannes, 28 Van Goghs, 21 Gauguins, and 17 Seurats, and attracted 47,000 visitors during the first month. Until this significant moment not one museum in Manhattan owned a single canvas by these artists, most of whom had been dead for forty years. Despite the Armory Show of 1913, America was still hostile to modern art.

In 1939, Mrs. John D. Rockefeller, Jr. and her husband (who hated modern art) deeded to the museum the land for its present buildings. All in all, she gave the museum 2,000 objects of art—190 paintings, 1,630 prints, 137 drawings, and 44 pieces of sculpture. Lillie P. Bliss also left the museum the greater part of her masterpieces by Cézanne, Matisse, Picasso, Seurat, Redon, Gauguin, and other artists. When Mary Sullivan died, her collection was auctioned at the Parke-Bernet Galleries. One painting by Derain was bought by Mrs. Rockefeller and given to the museum in memory of Mrs. Sullivan.

During the 1930's the collections grew through acquisition funds made possible by Mrs. Simon Guggenheim, whose generosity has continually provided the largest purchase fund for works of exceptional importance. Mainly through the generosity of some nine hundred donors, the museum has acquired the most important collection of twentieth-century painting and sculpture in the world.

The collections have grown from 2,600 items to nearly 20,000 works of art. Among its finest and most popular examples of paintings are Picasso's "Les Demoiselles d'Avignon" and the antiwar "Guernica," Rousseau's "The Dream," Matisse's "The Moroccans" and "The Dance," Marc Chagall's "I and the Village," Braque's "Woman with a Mandolin," Max Beckmann's "The Departure," Edward Hopper's "House by the Railroad" (the first painting acquired), Joseph Pickett's "Manchester Valley," Joan Miró's "Composition," Monet's "Water Lilies," and Jackson Pollock's "Number 1." The collections also include masterpieces by Bonnard, Toulouse-Lautrec, Cézanne, Kandinsky, Modigliani, Mondrian, Nolde, Léger, Rouault, Shahn, Tchelitchew, Van Gogh, Weber, Gorky, De Kooning, Magritte, Newman, Wyeth, Davis, Vasarely, Rothko, and Albers—to name just a very few.

Paintings by Still, Gottlieb,
and Kline (left to right).

In sculpture the museum excels in works by Constantin Brancusi, Alexander Calder, Edgar Degas, Gaston Lachaise, Jacques Lipchitz, Henry Moore, Auguste Rodin, David Smith, Marino Marini, Aristide Maillol, Julio Gonzalez, and Naum Gabo.

The museum's collections are arranged to help the visitor to understand modern art. The great innovations in style, technique, subject matter, and aesthetic goals that characterize modern art may be seen in about forty galleries on the second and third floors. These permanent collections progress in simple, well-defined categories of art periods, with works of a particular artist often grouped to show significant periods of development.

By starting on the second floor and following the conveniently num-
bered galleries, you will progress chronologically from the founders of modern painting to the Impressionists, Post-Impressionists, Anti-Impressionists, Neo-Impressionists, the Fauves, the German Expressionists, the Americans, Early and Late Cubists, Italian Futurists, Ex-

pressionist Abstractionists, Geometric Abstractionists, and Primitive Realists.

Separate galleries on this floor are devoted to Matisse, Léger, Monet's "Water Lilies," and the Philip L. Goodwin Galleries of Architecture and Design. These collections include architectural material, graphic design, furniture (especially chairs), and industrial objects. Some of the twentieth-century designs include Thonet bentwood chairs, Art Nouveau Tiffany glass, Bauhaus textiles, Machine Art, Kitchenware, Tableware, and Crafts. Among the designers are Ludwig Mies van der Rohe, Marcel Breuer, Alvar Aalto, Eero Saarinen, and Charles Eames. The collection comprises over a thousand examples selected for quality and historical significance.

The third-floor galleries continue with the late nineteenth-century and end with works which, in a manner of speaking, just came from the artists' studios and are hardly dry enough to stick to the pages of contemporary art history. In these galleries you begin with the movement toward the fantastic (di Chirico), and progress through Dada (Duchamp), the Surrealists (Dali), Picasso after 1930 ("Guernica"), the Realists (Wyeth) and Romantics after 1940, and the first-generation Abstract Expressionists.

Nearly a third of the galleries are devoted to the postwar Americans classified loosely as the New York School of Painting (or Action Painters), which includes Jackson Pollock, Hans Hofmann, Clyfford Still, Bradley Walker Tomlin, Franz Kline, Willem de Kooning, Robert Motherwell, Mark Rothko, Adolph Gottlieb, Ad Reinhardt, Mark Tobey, Alphonse Ossorio, and Philip Guston. (See *The Artist's World,* Dutton 1961, for more information on this group.)

Two galleries are devoted to second-generation Abstract Expressionists, Hard Edge Abstractionists, Pop Art, Op Art, kinetic constructions, combines, collages, assemblages, and so on. There are works by Jasper Johns, Robert Rauschenberg, Robert Indiana, Ellsworth Kelly, Alexander Liberman, Alfred Jensen, Andy Warhol, Claes Oldenburg, George Brecht, Richard Anuszkiewicz, and George Segal.

The new works on view in these galleries have had a profound influence on art communities throughout the world. It is admitted among authorities that these postwar American artists, and the daring judgment, evaluation, and selections of Alfred H. Barr, Jr., now Director of Collections, has made New York the art capital of the world.

The sculpture galleries are also chronologically arranged by style. There are nine works by Brancusi. The categories show Objects in Relation to Light, Idealized Objects, the Purified Object, as well as ex-

A collection of Tiffany Glass.

amples of Cubism, Futurism, Objects Constructed on Geometric Prin-
ciples, and Surrealist Sculpture. There are also works by Seymour
Lipton, Theodore Roszak, Ibram Lassaw, Isamu Noguchi, and Richard
Lippold. A number of well-known sculptures, including Lachaise's
"Standing Woman," Rodin's "St. John," Matisse's "Four Reliefs of
Backs," are to be found in the Abby Aldrich Rockefeller Sculpture
Garden.

The Abby Aldrich Rockefeller Print Room, visited by appointment,
can be entered from the third-floor galleries. Her gift of 1,600 prints
formed the nucleus of this study collection, now grown to 7,000 | 81
original prints by some 800 artists from 55 countries. The collection
is supplemented by over 700 drawings, some on exhibition in the Paul
J. Sachs Galleries. The Edward Steichen Photography Center empha-
sizes the historic phases of photography. The museum has exhibited

Sculptures by Wilhelm Lehmbruck.

photographs since 1932, and it was the first art museum to accord photography a regular and important share of its program.

The Main Hall on the street level and the new Z-shaped galleries are confined to the changing exhibition program, a principal activity of the museum. The influence and magnitude of the institution's aesthetic experiments reach far beyond the art community. The "Responsive Eye" show of Optical Art, held in 1965, affected everything from fashions to fiction. The program has also presented complete exhibitions of the work of Hans Hofmann, Robert Motherwell, Jackson Pollock, and a number of Europeans. Some of the most important group shows have been the surveys assembled by Dorothy C. Miller, and called simply

Sculptures by Constantin Brancusi.

Examples of "Minimal Art."

A lecture tour at the Museum of Modern Art.

"14 Americans" (1946), "15 Americans" (1952), "16 Americans" (1959), as well as others of this type held every two or three years. The museum's other major programs cover the range of popular culture, including the presentation of vintage Hollywood films, such as *Intolerance, Duck Soup, The Invisible Man, King Kong, Citizen Kane,* and other classics that marked distinct stages of cinematic development. The educational program also embraces art classes, gallery talks, art lending services, poetry readings, concerts, and symposiums.

Today the museum's total annual attendance is about a million, or the total of its first ten years' attendance. Unlike most museums, it receives no city, state, or Federal funds, and is supported entirely by admissions, publication sales, earnings from endowments and contributions, and membership enrollments, of which there are now about 38,000.

The growth of the museum, its collections, exhibitions, and membership have produced an acute and chronic space problem. The first phase of expansion was the opening in May, 1964, of an enlarged sculpture garden and new galleries designed by Philip Johnson. The next phase will include expansion into the quarters left by the Whitney Museum on 54th Street, directly behind the Museum of Modern Art.

| 85

THE MUSEUM OF PRIMITIVE ART

Address: 15 West 54th St. (near 5th Ave.), New York, N.Y.
Phone: CI 6-9494

Days: Open Tuesdays through Saturdays, 12–5; Sundays, 1–5. Closed holidays.
Admission: Adults, $.50; students, $.25.

Subway: IND 8th Ave. "E" train or 6th Ave. "F" train to Fifth Ave. station (53rd St.).
Bus: 5th Ave. or 6th Ave. bus to 54th St.
Auto: Limited garage parking.

Special Events: Gallery talks Fridays at 3. Lectures as announced.

Membership: Annual fee $15.00 up. Privileges include admission pass, discount on publications, etc.

The founder and president of the Museum of Primitive Art is Nelson A. Rockefeller, financier and collector of both primitive and contemporary art and presently the Governor of the State of New York. The Rockefeller family formerly owned the two town houses in which the museum is located.

A nonprofit institution incorporated under a charter granted by the New York State Board of Regents, the museum is privately supported. It opened in February, 1957, and is the only museum in existence devoted entirely to the arts of the indigenous cultures of the Americas, Africa, and Oceania. The museum mounts four major exhibitions annually to show that the arts of primitive peoples are an integral part of the heritage of man. Dr. Robert Goldwater, the museum's director, is one of the first scholars to study the relation between modern and primitive art. Although an ancient Egyptian sculptor and a woodcarver in present day Africa might seem very different, both primitive artists have worked in cultures and societies where human endeavors were felt to be conditioned by the supernatural forces of gods, demons, and spirits. Works of art produced in primitive societies are religious objects, saturated with magical significance. This combination of aesthetic value with magical or religious significance distinguishes primitive arts from all other arts.

The museum has about 20,000 visitors a year. Its reference library of more than 12,000 books and periodicals on primitive arts and cul-

tures provides detailed information about their techniques, aesthetics, and evolution. The archives hold upward of 15,000 photographs. The museum regularly publishes monographs and papers of special interest as well as illustrated catalogues of its exhibitions, and books.

The exhibition galleries are on the parlor floor and in the basement of one house, while offices for the museum take up sections of both buildings. The displays are arranged simply, with specimens marked and grouped to show relationships. Since it is a small museum, all the exhibitions are carefully edited to bring out the significance of each period. Over thirty-five shows from its own collections or on loan have been held since the museum opened. There have been exhibitions of stone sculptures from pre-Spanish Mexico, bronzes from early African kingdoms, textiles and featherwork of the ancient Incas, and gigantic fetish figures from Oceania.

In a recent show, "Masterpieces from the South Seas," 105 wood sculptures were gathered from the museum's collections to show the

Slit-drum heads from New Hebrides, Melanesia.

diverse cultures and art styles of the Polynesians, Melanesians, and Micronesians. There were sacred objects from Australia, beautifully fashioned missile clubs from Fiji, and house posts, masks, and a twenty-five foot crocodile from New Guinea.

The museum's collections range from bone carvings made 20,000 years ago to wood sculpture from modern New Guinea.

THE GALLERY OF MODERN ART
including The Huntington Hartford Collection
Address: 2 Columbus Circle, New York, N.Y.
Phone: LT 1-2311

Days: Tuesday through Saturday, 11–7; Sunday and holidays, 12–6.
Admission: Adults $1.00; students $.50; children under 12 $.25.

Subway: (1) IRT 7th Ave. to 59th St. station; (2) IND 6th Ave. or 8th Ave. to Columbus Circle 59th St. station.
Bus: 8th Ave. bus to Columbus Circle.
Auto: West Side Highway to 57th St. exit, or north on 8th Ave. Garage parking.

Gift Shop: Postcards of art works, catalogues, and books on sale in the lobby.

Restaurant: Cocktails in Gallery lounge; complete meals in Gauguin Room.

Special Events: Film programs and lectures.

Membership: Annual fee from $15.00.

The Gallery of Modern Art is operated by the Foundation for Modern Art at a cost of about $580,000 a year and is classified as an educational institution by the State of New York. It receives a tax-exempt status under the laws of the Internal Revenue Bureau. The museum at last count had over 700 members, who paid from $15 to $500 each for their membership. Its most recent attendance figures are estimated at 500,000 annually. | 89

The owner of the museum is George Huntington Hartford, heir to the A&P food-chain fortune. He is a Harvard graduate, a decorated hero of the Coast Guard during World War II, and a philanthropist

and culture patron. Many of his ideas are highly controversial and are forthrightly expressed in his book *Art and Anarchy,* a discussion of "How the Extremists and Exploiters Have Reduced the Fine Arts to Chaos and Commercialism." His interest in art culminated with the opening of the museum in March, 1964, to house his own art collection.

This $7.4 million museum is isolated on a small island in Columbus Circle at the western entrance to Central Park and is surrounded by traffic on all sides. It is directly across from the Coliseum and it is in the same architectural genre. The building is ten stories high but there is no way of knowing from the outside, for there are no windows. In creating the building Edward Durell Stone, the famous American architect, bucked the trend of glass facades and designed a Vermont marble facade, with a fine strip of glass down each side. The building is slightly curved to conform to the odd plot on which it stands.

The building was both praised and damned by the architectural community. As one renowned critic said: "The building works well, poses no challenges, asks no questions and gives no controversial answers." Another critic of art and architecture complained about the museum's being completely closed in: "The building gives the distinct impression of being the Grant's Tomb of Columbus Circle. If painting and sculpture are supposed to have life, one wonders why they should be embalmed in this mausoleum."

Behind the cold white facade, the interiors, with walls paneled in mahogany, solid bronze doors, parquet floors, and luxurious carpets, all give a richly warm, almost homelike atmosphere to the galleries. Each of the floor plans is identical.

Exhibition galleries start on the fifth floor. As you come out of the elevator there is a large gallery with a small wing on either side; each room contains a small group of paintings. Two floors are generally devoted to the permanent collection of Huntington Hartford, while two others are set aside for the hanging of temporary exhibits, such as the retrospective shows devoted to the work of Maxfield Parrish, Lovis Corinth, Clemente Orozco, Pavel Tchelitchew, Salvador Dali, and Aubrey Beardsley. These temporary exhibits have gained wide attention and have attracted an appreciative public.

The permanent collection comprises about eighty late-nineteenth- | 91
and twentieth-century French and American paintings of modest distinction. It is claimed that Hartford first decided to build the museum and then began to assemble the collection. *Newsweek* magazine, when describing the collection after the museum first opened,

The Gallery of Modern Art; Edward Durell Stone, architect.

In one of the galleries.

said: "Victorian taste lies behind Hartford's miscellany of 19th-century landscapes, Pre-Raphaelite mythology, out and out academicism, and Utopian pinups." Salvador Dali has called the collection "Fireman's Art." Incidentally, an entire gallery is set aside for the display of Dali's huge painting called "The Discovery of America by Christopher Columbus," which was commissioned for the museum by Hartford.

"My museum represents the taste of the country more than any of them," Hartford once told a *New York Times* reporter while discussing modern art museums. But perhaps the attitude one should have in visiting this museum and its collection is best summarized in Huntington Hartford's own book: "Let us form our own opinions concerning art. Let us not be afraid to disagree with the experts. . . ."

92 | LIBRARY AND MUSEUM OF THE PERFORMING ARTS AT LINCOLN CENTER

Address: Lincoln Center Plaza North, 111 Amsterdam Ave. at 65th St.,
New York, N.Y. (2 entrances).
Phone: 799-2200

*"The Discovery of America by
Christopher Columbus" by Salvador Dali.*

Days: Weekdays, 10–9; Saturdays, 10–6. Closed Sunday.
Admission: Free.

Subway: IRT Broadway-7th Ave. to 65th St. station.
Bus: Broadway bus to 65th St. and Broadway.
Auto: Parking garage in Lincoln Center.

The Library and Museum of the Performing Arts, designed by Eero Saarinen, is in the new Vivian Beaumont building in the Lincoln Center architectural complex. The main entrance is on Amsterdam Avenue and 65th Street. Another entrance on the theatre plaza faces the central pool containing Henry Moore's monumental two-piece bronze sculpture.

The nucleus of the collection in this library was supplied by the main Reference Branch of the New York Public Library at Fifth Avenue and 42nd Street, where these archives were originally located. The research materials now at Lincoln Center comprise half a million books, pamphlets, periodicals, sheet music, scores, manuscripts, phonograph records, photographs, theatre programs, clipping files, scrapbooks of reviews, and memorabilia. A recent addition to the theatre collection are Florence Vandamm's prints and negatives of over 2,000 professional theatre productions between 1925 and 1950.

A unique section of the Library and Museum of the Performing Arts is the Rodgers and Hammerstein Archives of Recorded Sound, the first major sound library. It contains over 100,000 records that reflect the development of recorded sound from its beginnings to the present.

The library also contains the Dance Collection, the world's only archive devoted solely to the literature and iconography of the dance. The Music Division, covering classical, jazz, pop, musical comedy, and experimental ventures, contains over 200,000 volumes.

The museum section is primarily for semipermanent and loan exhibitions of material from library collections, other Lincoln Center institutions, and the collections of other New York City museums. It has been suggested that the museum also house and exhibit the Society of Strings collections of great and rare violins.

The Main Gallery is devoted to thematic exhibitions dealing with various aspects of the arts. The Astor Gallery features exhibitions of autograph scores, original costume designs, models for dance productions, and manuscripts. The gallery was dedicated by Mrs. Vincent Astor in memory of her late husband, who played a major role in the development of the New York Library. The Amsterdam Gallery is devoted to various art exhibitions.

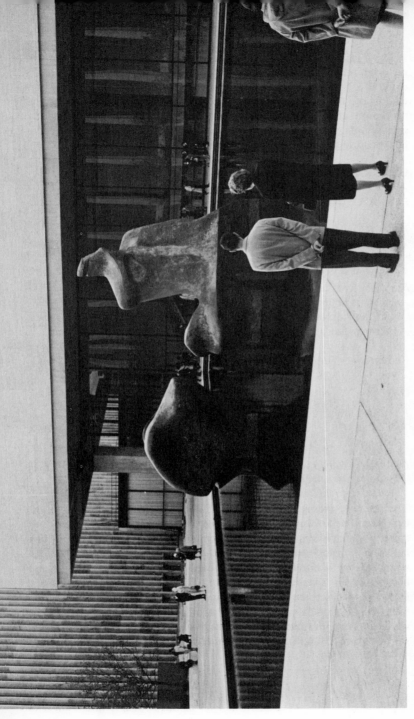

Henry Moore's great bronze sculpture dominates the plaza in front of the museum.

The Plaza entrance gallery houses exhibits, and has a gift shop of material related to the performing arts. The Mezzanine contains a children's library intended to develop a child's interest in, and appreciation of, the performing arts. The Heckscher Oval is a functional playhouse area where children attend story hour, Punch and Judy shows, fairs, festivals, and other activities for the pleasure and education of young people.

CENTRAL PARK ZOO

Address: 64th St. and Fifth Ave., New York, N.Y.
Phone: RE 4-1000

Days: Open daily. Buildings open 11–5.
Admission: Free.

Subway: BMT Astoria train to 60th St. station. North 4 blocks.
Bus: 5th Ave. or Madison Ave. to 64th St.
Auto: Two hours' free parking in Central Park Boathouse and Rambles parking lots behind zoo. Commercial garages on crosstown streets between 5th and Park Aves.

Restaurants: Terrace Cafeteria and Outdoor Café: hot dishes, sandwiches, snacks. Carretinas: snacks, soft drinks. Beer garden.
Gift Shop: Toys and small souvenirs at carretinas near sea-lion pool.
Feeding Times:

| Monkeys | 11 | Bears | 1:45 |
| Sea Lions | 1:30 | Lions | 2:00 |

Children's Facilities: Pony cart rides $.25. Children's Zoo: Open daily, 10:30–5. Admission $.10. Gift shop in zoo.

The interest, excitement, and charm of the zoo lie only partly in the exhibits. Visible also on any day are the many strata of New York society—the visitors from foreign lands in native dress, very proper ladies and gentlemen, stiff-backed and starched nannies, bearded strangers, mini-skirted teen-agers, young lovers, and mobs of scrambling children. Eventually everyone in New York goes to the Central Park Zoo—to see the lions, the tigers, sea lions, and monkeys.

In the fascinating monkey house are the forever-swaying gibbon of southeast Asia; the fantastic red-nosed, white-eyed, Halloween-masked, goat-bearded Mandrill; South American spider monkeys; Guinea

96 |

Feeding time for the sea lions at Central Park Zoo.

baboons with their piercing screech; the sloe-eyed white-crowned West African mangabey; and the stump-tail monkey from Malay; and the orangutan, a large, long-armed anthropoid ape that is less closely related to man than are the gorilla and chimpanzee.

The Central Park Zoo has its share of lions, tigers, jaguars, leopards, pumas, African camels, elephants, and rhinos. But the most fun at the zoo usually is watching the sea lions being fed every afternoon in the center pool below the terrace restaurant.

At the Terrace Cafeteria and Café the food is above average City Park Department fare. The chief virtue of the café is the vantage point it offers to viewers of the passing scene. Seats are at a premium both in winter and summer.

Another principal attraction is the Herbert Lehman Children's Zoo. Old McDonald's Farm, Three Little Pigs, Alice's White Rabbit, and other storybook figures appear in an imaginative setting where city children may encounter domesticated and farm animals in a warm and inviting way.

Children meet barnyard animals at the Children's Zoo.

This jovial whale delights children at the zoo.

The most recent addition to the zoo is the Delacorte clock, which is over the archway between the monkey house and the lion and tiger house. It has bronze monkeys that tell the hours by striking a big bell.

ABIGAIL ADAMS SMITH HOUSE

Address: 421 East 61st St. (at York Ave.), New York, N.Y.
Phone: TE 8-5489

Days: Mondays to Fridays, 10–4. Closed August 1st to Labor Day.
Admission: Free.

Subway: (1) IND 8th Ave. to 59th St. station, then crosstown 57th St. bus to York Ave. (2) IRT Lexington Ave. to 59th St. station, then bus as above.
Bus: 1st Ave. bus to East 61st St.
Auto: North on First Ave. or East River Drive to 61st St. exit. Ample parking lots.

This landmark was originally a carriage house on the estate of Colonel William Stephens Smith, aide-de-camp to George Washington and husband of Abigail Adams, the daughter of President John Adams.

The house is set on a high embankment about ten feet above 61st Street. Because it is located so far east the house is familiar mainly to the drivers taking the 61st Street exit off the East River Drive.

The estate once known as "Smith's Folly" dates to 1795. The original

Abigail Adams Smith House.

23-acre property with its huge mansion facing the East River was considered one of the finest estates in Manhattan. A map of the farm from a survey in 1806 by Joseph F. Mangin is in the New-York Historical Society.

In the early 1900's the property was purchased by the Colonial Dames of America, who have made it their headquarters and maintain the exhibition rooms—a music room, dining room, bedrooms, and parlors. Most of the authentic furnishings date from 1810 to 1820.

THE ASIA HOUSE GALLERY

Address: 112 East 64th St. (between Park and Lexington Aves.), New York, N.Y.

Phone: PL 1-4210

Days: Open weekdays, 10–5; Saturdays and holidays, 11–5; Sundays, 1–5.

Admission: Free.

Subway: IRT Lexington Ave. to 68th St. station. South 4 blocks.

Bus: Madison Ave. or Lexington Ave. to 64th St.
Auto: Limited street parking.

Gift Shop: Catalogues of gallery shows on sale.

Membership: Membership privileges include attendance at lectures, reception of publications, etc. Membership fees are $10–$25.

The modern Asia Society building, designed by Philip Johnson, is situated between Victorian brownstones on a tree-shaded residential street. The front of the building is faced entirely with a charcoal-colored glass. From the street the façade appears opaque, but from inside the building the glass is translucent. The building has seven floors. The library and lounge are on the first floor, the huge thirty-five by sixty-foot Gallery is on the second; and the 170-seat lecture hall and auditorium are in the basement, all open to the public. The third floor is occupied by the offices of the Japan Society, and the remaining floors by the Asia Society.

The Asia Soicety is "a non-profit, non-political membership organization founded in 1957 in the belief that there is a continuing need for greater knowledge of Asia among Americans." The society sponsors programs dealing with the cultural heritage of Asia. Covering contemporary economic, political, and social questions, these programs are given by the society's various Country Councils. Each council is composed of Americans familiar with a particular Asian country. The Country Council programs are open to the membership and invited guests in the Lecture Hall. The society also presents films, and dance and music recitals.

The Asia House Gallery exhibits the arts of Asia. It presents three loan exhibitions each year. Exhibitions have dealt with Rajput paintings, tea taste in Japanese art, the art of Nepal, and relics of ancient China. Tape-recorded half-hour lectures by the gallery director, designed to enlarge the viewer's understanding of each exhibition, may be rented by visitors for a small sum.

The Asian Literature Program acts as an unofficial and unpaid literary agency for Asian writers by encouraging American book and magazine editors to publish their works. This program handles more than three hundred manuscripts and proposals a year. The society has also developed the Asia Library, a series of books designed to acquaint the general reader with basic historic and contemporary facts on Asian nations.

In the Education Department American teachers are invited to improve their knowledge of Asian peoples and cultures. The department offers free literature and a course on the peoples and cultures of Asia. The Information and Reference Service answers general questions on Asian topics, and maintains a service for Asian visitors to enable them to make professional and business contacts while visiting New York.

THE FRICK COLLECTION
Address: 1 East 70th St. (corner of 5th Ave.), New York, N.Y.
Phone: BU 8-0700

Days: Open daily, 10–6; Sundays and major holidays, 1–6. Closed Mondays. Special summer hours; telephone museum.
Admission: Free. Children under 10 not admitted. Group visits by appointment only.

Subway: IRT Lexington Ave. to 68th St. station. East to 5th Ave.
Bus: 5th Ave. or Madison Ave. bus to 70th St.
Auto: North on Madison or Park Aves. Limited street parking.

Gift Shop: Postcards, reproductions, greeting cards for sale in lobby.

Special Events: From October to May illustrated lectures every Wednesday at 3. Sunday-afternoon chamber music concerts during the winter. Daily organ "interludes" at 11:30, 2:30, and 4:30.

Special restriction: Absolutely no cameras allowed.

The building housing the Frick Collection is a fine example of how people of extreme wealth lived in New York in the early part of this century. It is one of the few museums specifically built as a residence. With slight variations to accommodate the public, the mansion was opened as a museum in 1935. It appears much as it was when Henry Clay Frick, the steel magnate, lived there. It was built in 1913 by Carrere & Hastings, who specialized in French Classic Eclectic, and | 103 was occupied until 1931, when Mrs. Frick died. The building replaced the Lenox Library, which formerly occupied the site.

The mansion is much like a Louis XVI château that might be seen in the Loire Valley. The first floor is the only one of the three open

Asia House; Philip Johnson, architect.

The Frick Collection.

to the public, and has about fifteen rooms, not including the enclosed garden court. There are about forty rooms in the entire house.

The priceless collection displayed in this magnificent house contains works of art bought by Henry Frick over a period of forty years, and bequeathed in trust to a board of trustees empowered to set up the collection and the house as a center for the study of art and kindred subjects. The financier, who grew up near Pittsburgh, began collecting art seriously on his first trip abroad in 1880 with his friend Andrew Mellon. By 1900, he had acquired about sixty pictures, principally of the Barbizon School. During the next few years he obtained his first old masters, and in the decade from 1900 formed the basic character of the collection. There were 131 paintings among the works bequeathed in 1919 to form the Frick Collection. Many additional paintings have been acquired by the trustees.

The collection, under the watchful eyes of twenty-six guards, is not arranged according to any rigid classification of date or school, but possesses a harmonious freedom that retains the intimate atmosphere of a private home. The entrance leads directly into the Colonnade Court. Originally an open courtyard, its arched glass roof was put on when the museum was remodeled under the guidance of John Russell Pope. At some time during a visit, most visitors find themselves enjoying sitting on a stone bench in this lovely court, hypnotically watching the bronze frogs spouting water into the fountain.

In the East Court are the portrait of Conde de Teba by Goya and Claude Lorrain's "Sermon on the Mount." Of the four portraits in the Oval Room, two are by Van Dyck and two by Gainsborough.

The masterpieces hanging in the West Gallery are colorfully set off by Turner's lemon-yellow scenes of Cologne and Dieppe. At the far end of the gallery hang Veronese's "Wisdom and Strength" and "Choice of Hercules." Rembrandt's "Self-Portrait" and portrait of

Paintings by 18th-century English artists.

The Colonnade Court at the Frick Collection.

"Nicolaes Ruts," Velasquez's "Philip IV," and El Greco's "Vincente Anastagi" are highlights of the gallery. In the small Enamel Room are French painted enamels of the late fifteenth, sixteenth, and seventeenth centuries, from the Limoges workshops of Nardon Pénicaud and others.

The spacious wood-paneled library has a number of paintings by Gainsborough, Reynolds, Romney. Lawrence, Constable, and Turner. Over the mantel is a portrait of Henry Clay Frick. The porcelains are Chinese vases, chiefly the type known as Black Hawthorn. Some of the furniture is Queen Anne. In the Living Hall are "St. Jerome" by El Greco and "St. Francis" by Giovanni Bellini. The former hangs between two Holbeins, the latter between two Titians.

The Fragonard Room contains magnificently colored panels representing the Progress of Love that Madame du Barry commissioned for her pavilion at Louveciennes. In the Boucher Room a set of eight wall panels depicts cherubic figures impersonating the sciences and occupations of man. These were created by François Boucher to decorate the boudoir of Madame de Pompadour's château.

An unusual feature of the mansion is the massive organ, set near the stairs leading to the upper floors. It is played three times a day.

THE WHITNEY MUSEUM OF AMERICAN ART

Address: 945 Madison Ave. (at 75th St.), New York, N.Y.
Phone: 249-4100

Days: Open daily, 11–6; Sundays, noon to 6.
Admission: $.50. Children under 12 free.

Subway: IRT Lexington Ave. to 77th St. station. West to Madison Ave., south to museum.
Bus: Madison Ave. or 5th Ave. bus to 75th St.
Auto: North on Madison Ave. or Park Ave. Metered street parking.

Restaurant: Small cafeteria, light luncheon.

Gift Shop: Museum catalogues, selected art books, some reproductions and postcards.

The scope of the Whitney Museum of American Art is confined to painting, sculpture, and graphic arts of the United States created after 1900. Anyone viewing the collections will find the significant developments in American art from "The Eight" to the first wave of Modern Painting, Figurative artists of the 1920's, the Social Realists, the Hard-Edge Abstractionists, Magic Realists, New Abstractionists, New Naturalists, New Figurative painters, New Realists, and all the other schools that helped create rather than conserve a tradition that has put the Whitney in the front ranks of American museums.

Whitney Annuals are considered the most significant surveys and forecasts of trends in American art. Over the years more than 1,500 artists have appeared in the shows. The museum has never awarded prizes or medals. It believes that first-, second-, or third-place awards are arbitrary and meaningless, misleading to the public and unfair to the artists. Instead of awarding medals, the Whitney buys works of art, a policy that has had a wide influence on other museums. In most of its exhibits works are for sale, and no commission is charged. In addition to the Annuals, there are shows built around a particular school, period, subject, region, or talent.

The museum is open to the new, young, and experimental; it has | 107
always regarded the artist as the prime mover in aesthetic matters, and has respected artistic individuality. The museum makes its purchases through a small committee, and more than once has saved many an artist from a financial crisis.

*In the fourth floor
gallery with Breuer's
giant trapezoidal window
at the back.*

Visible proof of the museum's exciting growth is its superb new building on Madison Avenue, its third major move since it was officially opened in 1931. Gertrude Vanderbilt Whitney, a wealthy sculptor, founded and endowed the museum. She first showed the work of fellow artists in her MacDougal Alley studio in Greenwich Village. Later she converted an adjoining house at 8 West 8th Street into a gallery to hold regular exhibitions. Mrs. Whitney also allotted funds

| 109

*The Whitney Museum of American Art;
Marcel Breuer, architect.*

The entrance ramp at the Whitney.

to send promising artists abroad and to purchase their works. She was, in a sense, a one-woman foundation for the arts.

In 1915 she formed the Friends of the Young Artists to give youthful talent in this country an opportunity to show its work under a system without juries or prizes. Instead, works of art were purchased. Those purchases form the nucleus of the present Whitney Collection. By 1918 the Whitney Studio Club on 8th Street had been organized as an exhibition center. At the clubhouse, 147 West 4th Street, artists met

Another view of the ramp
and the sculpture court beneath.

socially and to plan, discuss, and execute their vigorous campaign to persuade the public to buy works of art from living Americans. The only requirement for admission to the club was talent; any serious artist who was introduced by a member could join. Membership included the leading young independent artists; eventually the club grew to a membership of over three hundred.

From 1916 to 1930 the artists who exhibited at the Whitney Studio Club did become the heroic figures in American art—John Sloan, Stuart Davis, Edward Hopper, Joseph Stella, William J. Glackens, Reuben Nakian, Reginald Marsh, Ernest Lawson, Walt Kuhn, Guy Péne duBois, Charles Demuth, and dozens of others. From almost every exhibit Mrs. Whitney bought works for her collection. Annuals were held from the beginning, and so grew in size, quality, and scope that by the middle twenties the Whitney Club was the most active and influential center of liberal art in the country.

By 1928 the club had achieved victory in the fight to gain acceptance for young artists with fresh ideas about art, and it disbanded. Twenty years later, in 1948, a similar organization, also called "The Club," was formed by the generation of Postwar Abstract Expressionists. At its peak, about 130 artists belonged. The Club did not hold exhibitions, but conducted a perpetual Friday-night dialogue from season to season. Its dedication was to promote the acceptance of Abstract Expressionist paintings in America. By the early sixties it became evident that there had been a breakthrough, and, like the club before it, this one, too, saw a great rebellion come full circle. In 1962, without quarters and interested younger members to assume leadership, The Club automatically dissolved, unable to absorb the psychological impact caused by the death of one of its leaders, Franz Kline. Achievements of both clubs are evident in the galleries at the Whitney.

After the Whitney Studio Club disbanded, the Whitney Museum opened on 8th Street on November 18, 1931, with Gertrude Whitney's collection of over five hundred art works. The museum's activities were much the same as today: to hold exhibitions, acquire works for the permanent collection, lend works to other institutions, and publish works on American art. The publication program has produced extensive catalogues, monographs, and broad histories by Director Lloyd Goodrich and associate John I. H. Bauer. The museum is maintained by the income from an endowment left by Mrs. Whitney. It does not receive any subsidy from the government, nor does the museum have a regular membership.

The Whitney was a landmark in Greenwich Village for twenty-five years, its quarters providing an atmosphere of intimacy and charm. But then it moved uptown. In a benevolent gesture, John Hay Whitney, Nelson A. Rockefeller, and Stephen C. Clark of the Museum of Modern Art offered land on West 54th Street for a new museum building. It opened in 1954. It was never large enough to handle the greatly increased number of visitors, caused in part by the juxtaposition of the two museums, which were back to back. On 8th Street the average attendance at the Whitney had been about 70,000 persons a year; on 54th Street it increased by 200,000.

In late September 1966 the Whitney moved to its spectacular new building designed by Marcel Breuer, architect of the UNESCO Headquarters in Paris. This magnificent structure has very much the appearance of a gigantic work of sculpture. It is a five-story, inverted pyramid of flame-treated gray granite and concrete, punctuated with seven fascinating sculptural windows of random size. The museum has 30,000 square feet of exhibition space with movable floor-to-ceiling partitions, making it possible to create a wide variety of space patterns for exhibition purposes. The floors are made of flagstone for more comfortable walking, and the floodlights are equipped with diffusion lenses and tiny mirrors to spread the light evenly on the art objects.

Sculpture by John Chamberlain (left foreground), *Marisol* (right), *and Lee Bontecou* (rear wall).

Paintings by Joseph Albers (left),
Kenneth Noland (top),
and Robert Rauschenberg (right),
and sculpture by James Wines (foreground)
exhibited at the opening of the new Whitney Museum.

One enters the building by crossing a concrete bridge, constructed over a sunken sculpture garden, into the street-level lobby. In the words of Ada Louise Huxtable, architectural critic for *The New York Times:* "Mr. Breuer's stark and sometimes unsettling structure may be less than pretty, but it has notable dignity and presence, two qualities not found uniformly in today's art. . . . The building has an extraordinary urbanity, which masquerades as a kind of 'back-to-structure' crudeness. . . . It stresses masses of stone, largely unpolished—in this case

Relaxing in a gallery.

a truly beautiful gray granite outside and in—raw concrete complete with board marks of the forms, rugged bush-hammered concrete aggregate for interior walls, bluestone and split-slate floors." There is an auditorium on the second floor for special events, such as lectures and symposiums, and there is a public restaurant on the lower level. The new building was formally opened with a splendid retrospective exhibition called "Art of the United States: 1670–1966," showing 365 works by 275 painters and sculptors.

FINCH COLLEGE MUSEUM OF ART
Address: 62 East 78th St. (near Park Ave.), New York, N.Y.
Phone: BU 8-8450

Days: Tuesdays through Sundays, 1–5. Closed Mondays.
Admission: Free.

Subway: IRT Lexington Ave. local to 77th St. station. Walk north one block, west to museum.

Bus: Madison Ave. or 5th Ave. bus to 77th St.
Auto: North on Park Ave. Metered street parking.

The Finch College Museum of Art is based on a simple educational premise: "If you expose anyone to great music or art for a while, he will develop an appreciation for it." This explanation was given by Ronald R. DeMarco, president of Finch College, shortly after he started the museum in 1959. "We had a twofold aim," he states: "one, of providing a setting in which our own students could become familiar with great paintings in the course of everyday living, the other serving the community with exhibitions of art not usually shown to the public." Some of these exhibitions have been "Pre-Christian Sculpture from Guerrero," "Art in Process," "Swedish Watercolors," "Genoese Painters," "Still-Life Painters," and "Master Drawings." The museum also has a modest acquisition program.

Finch, an exclusive girls' college on the fashionable Upper East Side, has allotted three floors in two of its brownstone buildings to its museum. There are two sections: an Old Master's Wing and a Contemporary Study Wing. The museum's rooms are the scene of college receptions, club meetings, and informal classes. The Contemporary section was especially designed for the leisurely study of work on exhibit and the artist's notes, drawings, preliminary sketches, photographs of characteristic work, and pertinent literature.

The museum forms an integral part of the college's art-study program. In addition to the basic art courses it offers—oriental, classical, and medieval art, Renaissance and baroque architecture and sculpture, and so on—the college teaches "Art Museum and Gallery Management," given by the museum's directors, Robert A. Manning and Elayne H. Varian. Special emphasis is laid on documentation, authentication, and presentation of art. The Finch College Museum serves as the laboratory for the course.

The school's art training program also has an Intercontinental Study Plan that gives students an opportunity to become acquainted with art in Europe by visiting museums, galleries, and architectural masterpieces in Paris, Florence, Toledo, Rome, and other important art centers.

| 117

Finch College Museum of Art.

THE LIBRARY OF PRESIDENTIAL PAPERS

Address: 17 East 80th St. (near Madison Ave.), New York, N.Y.
Phone: 249-1200

Days: Monday-Friday, 9–5.
Admission: Call for an appointment.

Subway: IRT Lexington Ave. to 77th St. station. West to Madison
Ave., north to 80th St.
Bus: 5th Ave. or Madison Ave. bus to 80th St.
Auto: North on Madison Ave. or Park Ave. Metered street parking.

The latest contribution to the growing cultural archives of New York
City will be in a $350,000 six-story limestone town house in the heart
of the museum and art-gallery section. The mansion that will house the
Library of Presidential Papers was formerly the home of financier Paul
M. Warburg and more recently New York University's Institute of
Fine Arts. The founding group, which includes a cosmetics manufacturer, a publisher, a philanthropist, a public-relations official, and an at-
torney, chose New York because of its concentration of scholars and
libraries, massive population, and transportation facilities. Former
Mayor Robert F. Wagner has recently agreed to become a member of
the Board of the library.

The library will collect original documents and reproductions of all
existing papers of all the Presidents. The collections will be indexed
and stored in the library, where reading and study rooms will be available to scholars. By means of these archives the library hopes to
facilitate the study of history by providing a central source of information, thereby eliminating the necessity of traveling throughout the
United States to individual presidential libraries.

Copies of documents will be available for loan to other libraries,
educational institutions, and individual scholars unable to visit the
building. A nominal fee will be charged for this service. A series of
lectures and meetings with government figures will give anyone interested a chance to learn about politics from practicing politicians. Some
scholarships will enable university graduates to serve internships in
particular fields of government at Federal, state, or local level. The
library also plans to produce exhibits for young students that will
"stimulate interest in the Presidency by recalling the details of the man
who held the job." These exhibits will be lent to other institutions.

As "tangible evidence of the evolving, changing and important nature

118 |

The Library of Presidential Papers.

of the papers and memorabilia in which it deals, the library will pro- | 119
vide for the President and the Vice President of the United States
special office space for themselves and their top assistants so that there
will be in New York a convenient and appropriate place for official
presidential functions to be carried out."

THE METROPOLITAN MUSEUM OF ART
Address: 5th Ave. and 82nd St., New York, N.Y.
Phone: TR 9-5500

Days: Open weekdays, 10–5; Sundays and holidays, 1–5.
Admission: Free.

Subway: IRT Lexington Ave. to 86th St. station. Walk three blocks west to 5th Ave., south to museum.
Bus: 5th Ave. or Madison Ave. bus to 82nd St.
Auto: North on Madison Ave. or Park Ave. Museum parking lot for visitors open daily, fee $1.00.

Restaurant: Museum has cafeteria-style restaurant at end of corridor to the left of main entrance. Complete luncheons, snacks. Open Monday through Saturday, 11:30–2:30; Sundays, 12–3. Coffee hours Saturday, 3–4:30; Sunday, 3:30–4:30.

Gift Shop: Art and book shop sells books, reproductions, silver, and jewelry. Well stocked with unique high quality art merchandise unobtainable in many commercial outlets.

Special Events: Afternoon and evening concerts, lectures. Gallery talks. Films.

Library: Art Reference Library open 10–4:45 Monday to Friday, open to qualified research workers and museum members. Photo and Slide Library, including sales of museum photographs, open 10–4:45 Monday through Friday.

Membership: Annual membership $15.00 up. Special privileges include ten free issues of museum bulletin, calendar, annual garden party at the Cloisters, library privileges, Saturday art classes, and other special activities for members' children.

120 | As a critic once said, the Metropolitan Museum of Art is the supermarket of American museums, where you can find enough art to satisfy any appetite. Although almost any segment of its contents could occupy a student or scholar for a generation of study and contemplation, the museum is particularly noted for its Egyptian, Greek, and Roman art, European paintings, arms and armor, and American paint-

The Great Hall of the Metropolitan Museum of Art.

Greek Sculpture of the 5th century B.C.

ings. Primarily a museum of retrospect, it also endeavors to relate its collections to the present and to the civilizations that produced the works of art.

The Metropolitan is the largest and most important treasure house of art in the United States and the fourth largest in the world—after the British Museum, Leningrad's Hermitage, and the Louvre in Paris. It contains the largest number of galleries (248), with the most floor space (20 acres), catering to astronomical annual attendances (6,281,-162), served by the biggest staff (670), with the most curators (128), making the most spectacular purchases ($2,300,000 for one painting), with the most impressive collections in the Western Hemisphere (365,000 works of art), and is also the richest by far ($104 million, excluding the art) of any museum in the United States.

The museum houses two concert halls, four restaurants, two photographic studios, four bookshops, three restoration laboratories, a photo-slide library, and a foundry with a complete set of seventeenth-century armorer's tools.

Because its collections are so overwhelming, it is impossible to see everything in a few hours or even days. The most sensible plan is to select just a few sections on which to concentrate during a single visit.

Following a somewhat straight and narrow route, a first tour could begin with the Cesnola group of Cypriote antiquities in the corridor at the left of the entrance, then on to the interior of the Peri-nebi tomb to the right of the entrance. Proceed from there to the Blumenthal Spanish patio, then down the hall to the hall of Medieval Sculpture to see the heroic wrought-iron Spanish choir screen, and then the Equestrian Court. On the second floor outstanding features are Rodin's "The Thinker" and the Arthur M. Sackler Far Eastern Gallery. The visit might close with a long look at the room containing twenty-five paintings by Rembrandt. One of them is the world-famous "Aristotle Contemplating the Bust of Homer," whose much publicized purchase price at auction ($2,300,000) makes it the second costliest work of art known to man. The costliest: Leonardo da Vinci's portrait of Ginevra de' Benci, purchased by the National Gallery of Art for over $5,000,000 from Prince Franz Josef II of Liechtenstein.)

Owing to the size of the Metropolitan and the number of people it attracts, these galleries alone could occupy a visitor for the better part of a long afternoon. The best place for some rest and refreshment is the canopied restaurant, formerly the old Roman Court, on the main floor.

The Metropolitan is divided into some thirteen curatorial departments, including the Cloisters at Fort Tryon, the Costume Institute, and the Junior Museum. The last two have their own entrances at the north and south wings along Fifth Avenue. The entire complex of buildings includes at least seventeen units, incorporating wings, galleries, many hallways, and historic houses. The museum's first structure, in 1874, has been added onto every ten or twenty years. When the museum opened, it owned no art, no building, and had no funds, and no provisions were made for the future. Since the first building plans were drawn, not a year has passed without some part of the structure being in the hands of an architect for redesigning, improvement, alteration, or addition.

At least twice in the past forty years responsible individuals have suggested that the building be abandoned. Solomon R. Guggenheim in 1933 offered a sizable donation toward a new building. During World War II the museum entertained the idea of moving, but Robert Moses, then Commissioner of Parks, made it clear that the Museum had to stay where it was. The land and building belong to the City of New York; the art collections belong to the Metropolitan.

Bas-relief from the palace of Ashurnasirpal II, King of Assyria (883–859 B.C.), at Kalhu (modern Nimrud).

When James J. Rorimer, the late Director of the Metropolitan, returned from service, he set out on a vast program to rehabilitate the museum. He not only made America more culture conscious, but vastly improved the archaic, dusty atmosphere of museums. His personal accomplishments are too numerous to mention, but many are visible to the museum visitor.

In 1967 Thomas P. F. Hoving, former Commissioner of Parks, was named Director. Previously he had been Curator of the Cloisters before going to the Parks Department. His responsibility as director of America's largest museum complex traverses the complete range of matters legal, financial, architectural, and curatorial. He is also

A portrait sphinx of Queen Hatshepsut, XVIII Dynasty (c. 1490–1480 B.C.).

The Equestrian Court.

responsible for the security of the collections, and personnel, engineering (including superintendence of the buildings), purchase of supplies, management of the membership program, production of publications, development of new installations and exhibits, operation of the library, the care of museum documents and archives, conservation, restoration, and for good measure, fund raising.

Through the munificent philanthropy of the Metropolitan's chief benefactors the collections have grown to their present scope and importance. Among these benefactors have been J. Pierpont Morgan, Benjamin Altman, Horace O. Havemeyer, Samuel P. Avery, Edward C. Moore, Julian X. Bache, Lord Carnarvon, John Taylor Johnston, William K. Vanderbilt, Isaac D. Fletcher, Theodore Davis, Mrs. Russell Sage, William T. Walters, Brayton Ives, Michael Dreicer, and Dr. Eugene Bolles. Growth still depends heavily on individual bequests and gifts from philanthropic citizens. Benefactors have also sponsored expeditions and excavations, such as those in Egypt that were handsomely supported by the generosity of Edward S. Harkness.

Egyptian art is displayed on the main floor, to the right of the entrance, beginning with the red granite Sphinx of Queen Hatshepsut and the tomb of Peri-nebi. The collection continues through about eight galleries, some of which are being renovated and reinstalled for chronological clarity. The collection reveals the civilization of the Nile Valley as it developed in an unbroken story of human progress, beginning some 6,000 years ago and lasting until Egypt was absorbed into the Roman Empire. The art objects found in these galleries reflect daily life, customs, and beliefs. It is the largest and most comprehensive Egyptian collection in America, and is complemented by the collections in the Brooklyn Museum.

The chronology of ancient Egypt is conveniently divided into thirty dynasties, each representing successive generations of ruling families. The dynasties are grouped into broad periods known as Early Dynastic, the Early Kingdom, the Old Kingdom, Middle Kingdom, New Kingdom, and Late Dynastic.

The most familiar example of Egyptian architecture in the museum is the tomb of Peri-nebi, Lord Chamberlain in the Fifth Dynasty. In 1913, almost 4,500 years after it was constructed, it was disassembled, and reconstructed in the museum. The arrangement of the complete tomb is shown in cutaway models.

In the galleries surrounding the massive sepulchre are funerary models from the tomb of the nobleman Meketre. Unearthed in Egypt, the miniature, brightly colored, carved figures appear to belong in a dollhouse. Intended to aid the nobleman in his life after death, the models are documentary evidence of daily life, showing the nobleman's tree-sheltered pool, his "yachts" on the Nile, servants harpooning fish, and scenes in a granary and carpenter shops.

The Egyptian jewelry collection is unequaled outside Cairo. In the same gallery, near the Grace Rainey Rogers auditorium, are displays of the toiletries of the ancient Egyptians: metal mirrors, bronze razors, little pots and jars for perfumes, rouge, and eye paint. A variety of tools represents various arts, crafts, and professions.

Some embalmed mummies are to be found in adjoining galleries. During the process of preparing a mummy, the body was disemboweled, cured or tanned, dehydrated with soda, and then packed with sawdust and wrapped in resin-soaked linens. Rolled in layer upon layer of bandages, sheets, and pads, the body was finally placed in the coffin, with the head facing the east.

*Monumental sculpture of a Bodhisattva
in polychromed sandstone from Shansi,
China, Northern Ch'i Dynasty, 550–577* A.D.

In the Egyptian Statuary Courtyard stand temple sculpture, sarcoph- agi, limestone reliefs, altars, offering tables, a papyrus capital, and a number of enormous standing, seated, and kneeling statues of Queen Hatshepsut. She was frequently portrayed in the garb of a man, includ- ing a ceremonial beard—because as a woman she was not qualified to rule. When she died her successor ordered all her monuments defaced and destroyed. The fragments were discoverd by the museum's expedi- tions of 1921, and were laboriously pieced together.

Ancient Near Eastern Art is reached through the Egyptian Statuary Courtyard. A large portion of one wall is covered with Assyrian relief sculpture. The arched doorway is guarded by two great human-headed beasts from the palace of Ashurnasirpal II, King of Assyria. The cuneiform inscriptions and figures in relief were worked by vigorous and expert sculptors in stone. An inscription states that Ashurnasirpal built the city of Kalhu (modern Nimrud) and that "in white limestone and alabaster I fashioned beasts of the mountains and of the seas and

South Italian red-figure vases, 4th century B.C.

set them up in its gates. I adorned it, made it glorious and put knobs all around it. . . ."

About a dozen galleries containing Greek and Roman art start at the left of the main entrance and lead directly to the museum restaurant. The upper and lower portions of a huge marble Ionic capital from the Temple of Artemis at Sardis are placed at the foyer of the restaurant. The hall arcade holds the important Cesnola collection of antiquities from Cyprus, acquired in 1874, that formed the beginning of the museum's collections. The stone and terra-cotta sculpture, vases, limestone reliefs, bronzes, gold jewelry, silver—more than five thousand items—were excavated by General Luigi Palma di Cesnola. An Italian soldier of fortune, he won his rank in our Civil War. He excavated in Cyprus while serving as the American consul there. He sold his collections of antiquities to the Metropolitan and became its first director in 1879, eight years after the state granted a charter to the museum. Recalling this colorful personality, the former curator of prints A. Hyatt Mayor wrote in the Museum *Bulletin*: ". . . since the General liked to find everybody alert and on the job, his shoes had steel heels that could be heard several galleries away. When his military tidiness was offended by the headless bodies and bodiless heads among the sculpture that he had dug up, he set any head on any body that it would approximately fit, plastering up the chinks in the necks with a paste of lime-dust and honey. The Cypriot gods and goddesses endured the mixture all winter, but when the windows were opened in summer they put on collars of flies."

The collection of Greek and Roman art continues in the galleries directly above, on the second floor. Comprising the work of several civilizations, Greek art, including Roman copies of Greek originals, is arranged by material, such as stone sculpture. Roman sculptures and paintings are displayed together. Gold, silver, glass, and coins are grouped by material without ethnic distinction, but Etruscan art is shown as an entity. There is an elegantly tarnished bronze chariot from a tomb in Spoleto, terra-cotta fragments, vases, and other Etruscan relics. The arts of Cyprus and Sardis, on the first floor, are confined to one gallery.

The earliest works of art in the museum are from the Cyclades, a group of islands in the Aegean Sea. Principally marble statuettes of women, these simple forms with arms bent at the elbows and held across the chest suggest peasant art. The Mycenaean period is represented by glossy black terra-cotta vases that show marine life and chariot scenes. The priceless collection of Greek pots contains some

1,450 items. The Greek Geometric period takes its name from the geometric vase patterns that contrast with the figurative decorations of the Mycenaean period. Most of these vases, such as the three huge kraters that served as tomb monuments, were used in burial rites.

Greek art made rapid advances in the techniques of rendering the human figure. The outstanding collection in the second-floor galleries shows Greeks at home, working, at play, at festivals, and at war, all depicted on the black- and red-figure vases of Attica. In one display case forty-five different vases have been assembled in an effective exhibit of storage and water jars; vases for cosmetics, oils, and perfumes; drinking cups; wine jugs, and bowls for mixing wine and water.

The earliest Greek marble statue in the museum, and one of the earliest extant, is the Archaic period figure of a young man, which probably stood over his tomb. A variety of styles and techniques in Greek coinage reveal the development of types and symbols—the Pegasus of Corinth, the Owl of Athens, the Tortoise of Aegina.

Marble imperial portrait sculptures from Rome are in the first gallery to the left of the main hall. The colossal portrait of Emperor Constantine marked a significant phase of Roman art, when the sculptor strove for an exact likeness of his subject. The museum owns the greatest group of Roman paintings to be seen outside Italy. Monumental frescoes from a villa at Boscoreale on Mount Vesuvius show rustic scenes and architectural cityscapes painted in the vivid red so often identified with wall paintings from Pompeii. The most impressive addition to the collection is a complete bedroom with magnificent frescoes and a tile floor.

The Blumenthal Patio and Thomas J. Watson Library are on the ground floor to the left of the main stairway. The library, with 155,000 volumes and over 1000 periodicals, contains the greatest independent reference and research collection of art publications in America. Entrance to the library is by way of the patio. The patio was brought from Spain in the early 1900's, and formed a magnificent inner hall in the George Blumenthal house at 70th Street and Park Avenue. Mr. Blumenthal was president of the museum from 1934 to 1941. When the house was torn down, shortly after his death, the entire patio was dismantled, and each marble carving, column, window, doorjamb, frame, and two thousand blocks of marble were stored in the museum. | 131

In the preparation of plans for the new wing to house the Watson Library, study rooms, and print collections, the patio was incorporated as the central feature, with areas connecting with the Library, Renaissance Art galleries on the first floor, and Print Gallery on the second

Colonial furniture of the 17th century in the American Wing.

floor. The opening of the patio marked a major accomplishment in the museum's redevelopment program.

This beautifully proportioned court follows as closely as possible its original appearance in the castle of the Fajardo family, near the southeastern coast of Spain. The original setting was poetically described by Olga Raggio, the museum's curator of Renaissance arts, who visited the site to secure the photographs and measurements necessary to the reconstruction in New York: "The traveler who, after having admired the beauties of Granada, braves the dusty road winding eastward through the desolate ranges of the Sierra Maria and reaches the village of Velez Blanco, discovers the svelte silhouette of the castle of

In the Blumenthal Patio.

French porcelains and furniture of the 18th century.

the Fajardos standing upon a rocky spur and dominating a vast plain. The warm yellow glow of its walls proudly rising against the stony gray mountains and the southern blue sky, the whitewashed houses of the village clustering at its foot, and the vast expanse of the valley, dotted with olive trees and vine groves, make a truly unforgettable sight."

In 1904, the owners of the castle decided to sell the marbles to a French interior decorator, who transported the pieces to Paris, where they were offered for sale to prominent American collectors. The richly carved Renaissance patio, a unique example of Spanish and Italian architecture, was first offered to Archer M. Huntington for possible use as a building to house the Hispanic Society of America, but without result. In 1913, George Blumenthal purchased the marbles for his New York mansion. From the time the patio left Spain until it was reinstalled in the Metropolitan, exactly sixty years had elapsed.

Medieval art is displayed in one of the enormous single galleries directly to the rear from the main entrance, reached by passing through either to the right or to the left of the stairs. The collection shows Early Christian art, Byzantine and Ottonian art, and Romanesque and Early Gothic sculpture and furniture. In the Tapestry Hall hang fourteen textile panels depicting the Sacraments of the Church with parallel scenes from the Old Testament. The immense Medieval Sculpture Hall is dominated by a breathtaking 45-by-47-foot wrought-iron choir screen, weighing 60,000 pounds, from the Cathedral of Valladolid, Spain. Made in 1668 to separate the choir from the congregation, this monumental example of Spanish ironwork, the only one of its type in a public museum, was a gift of the William Randolph Hearst Foundation. When the famous "Mona Lisa" (on loan from the Louvre in Paris) was displayed in the musem in 1963, it was placed against this three-story-high screen.

The Western European Arts section encompasses works of art made in Europe from the beginning of the Renaissance to the present. It is the largest and most varied department of the museum, with entire rooms from palaces, hotels, and country estates, together with all their accessories and furnishings from floor to ceiling. The objects illustrate the changes in taste and style that have succeeded one another for some five hundred years—early Renaissance, mannerism, seventeenth-century baroque, eighteenth-century rococo, neoclassicism, the period of Louis XVI, and so on.

European ceramics, glass, and metalwork are displayed on the ground floor, in fifteen galleries. To reach them, take the stairway in the Tapestry Hall. This vast collection of art offers French, German, and Dutch ceramics, eighteenth-century French and English silver, the art of Fabergé, gold lapidary work, early German timepieces, compasses, portrait miniatures, China trade porcelain, miniature silver sets, and Venetian glass. Rare examples of Medici porcelain, made in Florence about 1580, represent early European attempts to imitate Chinese porcelains.

Renaissance arts are displayed in ten galleries. The first gallery, chronologically, contains a bedroom from the Segredo Palace in Venice that is decorated with at least twenty-five cherubs on the walls and ceiling. Although early Renaissance architecture can be seen on a grand scale only in Italy, the Metropolitan has on view a small fifteenth-century chamber of intarsia work from the palace of the Duke of Urbino in Gubbio. A glazed terra-cotta altarpiece by Andrea Della Robbia, Italian bronzes, and a sedan chair are noteworthy in this section.

French furniture of the 17th century.

The twelve galleries of French art, to the left of the Medieval Sculpture Hall, also contain complete rooms with decorative accessories. As you walk through, you can see characteristic examples of extravagant decorative art. Signed works by the greatest French cabinetmakers of the late 1700's are in the Grand Salon from the Hôtel de Tesse at No. 1 Quai Voltaire, and one can also see a sumptuous bedroom of the Louis XIV period. A shopfront from 3 Quai Bourdon on the Île Saint-Louis displays Sèvres "Rose Pompadour" vases and objects from the Samuel H. Kress Foundation collection, together with superb examples of Louis XVI furniture inlaid with porcelain plaques painted with flowers by Martin Carlin, a master cabinetmaker who worked in Paris about 1766.

Eight galleries of English art form the last set of rooms entered directly from the West Lounge. In these galleries are assembled late-seventeenth- and eighteenth-century interiors. Each room contains a photograph of the English manor house from which it came. A stately dining room from Lansdowne House was designed by Robert Adam, one of England's leading architects and decorators. It is elegantly furnished with a crystal chandelier, life-size sculpture in the wall niches, and a mahogany dining table. A staircase carved by Grinling Gibbons in 1677 is the only known example of this type by the famous wood-carver.

Exhibits of arms and armor are reached by going straight back to the Tapestry Hall, then turning right. You are immediately confronted by a jousting knight, ready for the charge. The extraordinarily comprehensive collection in the Equestrian Court illustrates the technical and artistic evolution of weapons and protective equipment in Europe. Some of the armor was so ingeniously designed that it was virtually impregnable. A man's armor might weigh as much as eighty-five pounds; that of a horse, up to ninety-two pounds. The eight galleries surrounding the hall display swords, ceremonial spurs, kidney daggers, maces, crossbows, firearms, great basinets, helms, gauntlets, toe and elbow caps, and mail shirts tailored to fit the body loosely, but linked so closely that they could not be penetrated with a dagger. A unique tournament book of 126 watercolors shows how jousting armor was worn.

An outstanding example of the armorers' art is the parade suit of Henry II of France. It is estimated that a skilled metalworker would

| 137

A unique carved wooden staircase by Grinling Gibbons from 17th-century England.

have needed two years to accomplish the forging, embossing, dama-scening, leaf-gilding, silvering, punch work, and blueing done on the armor. It is truly fit for a king. Many pieces of armor are signed by the artisans. By turning right outside the gallery, you come to the section devoted to Oriental arms and armor.

The American Wing, a separate building easily reached through the gallery of armor, displays the early domestic arts of the United States. Twenty-five period rooms, removed from original dwellings, were brought to the museum and arranged chronologically on three floors.

The earliest examples of Colonial craftsmanship are displayed on the third floor in rooms covering the period 1640-1750. Gothic in-fluence on the construction of the central room is evident in the roughly hewn trusses and beams. The earliest American table known to exist, a trestle type of pin oak from New England, stands in the middle of the room.

The rooms on the second floor date from 1750 to about 1790. Char-acteristic of the era are the increasing use of mahogany, and the hand-cut leaves, flowers, vines, and naturalistic detail on highboys, lowboys, chairs, and tables. The main central gallery re-creates the assembly room from the City Tavern in Alexandria, Virginia, in 1793, then a major East Coast stopping place between North and South.

The first floor of the eighteenth- and early-nineteenth-century in-teriors is notable for the splendid Van Rensselaer Room taken from a great mansion built in Albany in 1765. The unusual English wallpaper, made especially for the room, consists of large panels of romantic landscapes and seacoast scenes encircled by a scroll frame. The Van Rensselaer house was a striking example of Georgian architecture in the Middle Atlantic Colonies.

American painting and sculpture are displayed on the balcony over-looking the Equestrian Hall. Many masterpieces figure prominently in the furnished rooms of the American Wing. A large number of im-portant American paintings that were acquired in the decades before 1900 form the nucleus of the collection.

The Metropolitan held an outstanding exhibition of its American Collection in 1965, when 425 paintings were on view in 22 galleries. With the exception of American paintings of the seventeenth century, the museum's collection of the work of native painters and sculptors is the most complete and significant in existence, touching on every artist and style important to the history and development of art in America. Owing to limitations of space, only a fraction of its 1,250 works by nearly 625 artists are on display. The extraordinary collection is de-scribed in detail in three very informative catalogues: *American Sculp-*

The Landsdowne Dining Room from 18th-century England.

"Odalisque en Grisaille" by
Jean Auguste Dominique Ingres.

ture, by Albert Ten Eyck Gardner; *American Paintings* (painters born by 1815), by Mr. Gardner and Stuart P. Field; and *American Painting in the 20th Century,* by Henry Geldzahler.

Far Eastern and Islamic art are on the second floor, directly above the balcony to the right. Chinese sculpture is impressively displayed in two large galleries named for Arthur M. Sackler, a collector of Oriental art. A spectacular fresco of a Buddha surrounded by his disciples dominates one gallery. Monumental heads and full figures of Buddha, one standing 14 feet high, of stone, bronze, and wood, date from the second century after Christ to the fourteenth century. A stone pagoda, considered the oldest and most important Chinese architectural monument in a Western museum, is carved with guardians, dragons, floral motifs, animal masks, and countless figures of Buddha.

The collection of Islamic art illustrates all major periods, and contains ceramics, glass, rugs, metalwork, woodwork, ivory carvings, and miniature paintings. Those sections are at present undergoing renovation and reinstallation.

Near Eastern and Far Eastern art are in the gallery directly above

American paintings and sculpture of the 19th century.

the Egyptian Sculpture Hall. Although the galleries are temporarily closed, visitors in limited numbers may easily secure passes at the Information Desk to visit the Heber R. Bishop Jade Collection, a selection of Chinese paintings, bronzes, ceramics, sculpture, Japanese screens, and Oriental rugs. While the galleries are being renovated, the works will continue to be seen, on request, in accordance with museum policy.

European paintings are displayed in the forty-five galleries beginning directly at the head of the stairs on the second floor. Over seven hundred masterpieces present the evolution of painting in Europe from the thirteenth century through the first quarter of the twentieth century. Byzantine, Spanish, Italian, Dutch, Flemish, British, French, and German paintings are arranged by historical periods and schools.

Among the great masters and works in the collections are: Benvenuto Cellini ("Rospigliosi Cup"), Franz Hals ("The Merry Company"), Rembrandt van Rijn ("Aristotle Contemplating the Bust of Homer"), Lucas Cranach ("The Judgment of Paris"), Peter Paul Rubens ("The Fox Hunt"), Nicolas Poussin ("Rape of the Sabine Women"), Georges de La Tour ("The Fortuneteller"), El Greco ("View of Toledo"), Michelangelo Caravaggio ("The Musicians"), Giovanni Paolo Pannini ("Renaissance Room"), Canaletto ("Scene in Venice"), Eugène Delacroix ("Abduction of Rebecca"), J. M. W. Turner ("The Grand Canal"), Jean Auguste Dominique Ingres ("Odalisque en Grisaille"), Edouard Manet ("Boating"), Vincent Van Gogh ("Portrait of the Artist"), Pablo Picasso ("Gertrude Stein"), and Paul Cézanne ("The Cardplayers").

The European collection personifies the multiple facets of the museum's personality. Its roles of presentation and use, education and entertainment give the institution a vitality evident the moment you step inside. Albert Ten Eyck Gardner described the museum's mission in its *Bulletin*: "Let us look at the art museum not as a collection of tangible artifacts, but rather as an expression of ideas and feelings about man and his most important work, art."

COSTUME INSTITUTE OF THE METROPOLITAN MUSEUM OF ART

142 | *Address:* 5th Ave. and 83rd St., New York, N.Y.
Phone: TR 9-5500

Days: Exhibition galleries open to the public during museum hours: weekdays, 10–5; Sundays, 1–5. Closed holidays. Research facilities open to Costume Institute members Monday to Friday, 10–5.

Admission: Free.

Subway: IRT Lexington Ave. to 86th St. station. Walk three blocks
west to 5th Ave., south to museum.
Bus: 5th Ave. or Madison Ave. bus to 83rd St.
Auto: North on Madison Ave. or Park Ave. Museum parking lot for
visitors open daily, fee $1.00.

Restaurant: See listing for Metropolitan Museum.

The Costume Institute of the Metropolitan Museum offers exhibits of
public interest that show the social, technical, and aesthetic values of
costumes. The "Vignettes of Fashion" on display are like department-
store mannequins in the windows of the best ladies' and gentlemen's
shops through the years. The groupings depict French, English, and
American costumes worn for daily occasions.

There are scenes showing costumes for the morning stroll, shopping,
a walk in the garden, a family visit, courtship, the bride, a family

The Costume Institute of the Metropolitan Museum.

musicale (in a Louis XVI drawing room), and an Edwardian parlor at teatime.

In addition to public exhibitions, the institute maintains Designers' Rooms, a Costume Study-Storage, and Millinery and Shoe Study Storage for members' use. These rooms contain thousands of authentic costumes and accessories gathered from all over the world. The collections are a practical source of inspiration for fashion designers, theatre directors, motion-picture and television wardrobe designers, and students. The Reference Library and Textile Study Room are available to the public by appointment.

The public galleries also display a collection of crimson and blue embroideries from the islands of Greece. Turbaned figures, peacocks, ewers, and tulips in these designs reveal Turkish influence. Near the 83rd Street entrance is the Mrs. William Randolph Hearst Collection of Fans. These eighteenth-century fans were made of ivory, mother-of-pearl, tortoiseshell, and other materials by skilled painters and craftsmen. One of the fans has a life-size oval face, with two holes for eyes through which the holder could peek. Ecclesiastical lace, collars, and robes are also displayed.

JUNIOR MUSEUM OF THE METROPOLITAN MUSEUM OF ART

Address: 5th Ave. and 81st St., New York, N.Y.
Phone: TR 9-5500

Days: Open weekdays, 10–5; Sundays and holidays, 1–5.
Admission: Free.

Subway: IRT Lexington Ave. to 86th St. station. Walk three blocks west to 5th Ave., south to museum.
Bus: 5th Ave. or Madison Ave. bus to 81st St.
Auto: North on Madison Ave. or Park Ave. Museum parking lot for visitors open daily, fee $1.00.

Restaurant: Snack bar; also see listing for Metropolitan Museum.

144

Lectures and Tours: For school groups.

Gift Shop: Well stocked with art merchandise especially suited to young people.

*Artifacts in a strata display
at the Junior Museum.*

The Junior Museum was established in 1941 and now occupies the entire South Wing on the first floor, with three entrances. It is a separate arm of the Metropolitan, pleasantly informal for children, who may roam through it freely. The main purpose of the Junior Museum is to contribute to the realization of the chartered purpose of the Metropolitan, "encouraging and developing the study of the fine arts . . . and furnishing popular instruction. . . ." In accomplishing this, the staff seeks to introduce children to the Metropolitan and to help them to know and enjoy its collections. It is confidently expected that these young people will be the students, artists, designers, architects, interested laymen, and perhaps patrons of the future.

Upon entering the building, children find a self-service checking rack for coats and parcels, supermarket carts for their box lunches, washrooms, and a registration desk. The lobby gallery that adjoins the Junior Museum, although not actually part of it, is planned with children's interests in mind. It is a gallery of architectural models of ancient Egyptian, Greek, and Roman buildings and casts of related masterpieces of sculpture.

The young visitors are well provided with a choice of activities and exhibits in the modern and spacious setting wherein the staff provides hospitality and interpretation. Usually there is one major exhibit, such as "The Age of Discovery," which began with Marco Polo and progressed through the opening of the New World. Another exhibit, "Archaeology and the World," showed archaeological tools and how artifacts were buried under layer upon layer of succeeding civilizations. The display was made vivid with an example of a cutaway section from lower Manhattan containing Indian remains at the lowest level, and progressing upward to the present time.

In addition to the many displays and exhibitions specifically scaled to the junior world, there are art classes, and Saturday programs that combine live performances, music, films, and demonstrations based on the collections. The Junior Museum also has a well-stocked and imaginatively decorated library, and a senior-size snack bar seating 204 children.

THE SOLOMON R. GUGGENHEIM MUSEUM

Address: 1071 5th Ave. (between 88th and 89th Sts.), New York, N.Y.

Phone: EN 9-5110

Days: Open daily, 10–6; Sundays and holidays, 12–6. Closed Mondays, except on holidays. Open Thursday evenings till 9.
Admission: $.50.

Subway: IRT Lexington Ave. to 86th St. station. Walk west to 5th Ave., north to museum.
Bus: 5th Ave. or Madison Ave. bus to 88th St.
Auto: North on Madison Ave. or Park Ave. Limited street parking.

Gift Shop: Publications, catalogues, and reproductions for sale in lobby.

Membership: Annual fee $100.

The Solomon R. Guggenheim Museum;
Frank Lloyd Wright, architect.

During the next few years, the Guggenheim Museum will acquire a three-and-a-half-story annex, and its spiraling ramp will be punctuated by little doorways serving as entrances to each new floor. After some juggling of administrative offices and exhibition galleries to install the Justin K. Thannhauser collection of seventy-five paintings, the new annex will provide much-needed space for the museum's collection of over 4,000 works of art.

At present the collection contains works from the late nineteenth century to the present. It excels in early abstractions. Kandinsky is represented by more than 130 paintings. Paul Klee, Franz Marc, Robert Delaunay, Albert Gleizes, Marc Chagall, Laszlo Moholy-Nagy, and Fernand Léger are some of the twentieth-century masters owned by the Guggenheim. In sculpture the collection owns works by Alexander Calder, Aleksandr Archipenko, and Constantin Brancusi, among others. The acquisition program, as Thomas M. Messer, the director, points out, is largely shaped by the tastes and preferences of successive generations of directors and the attitudes of the ever-changing groups of trustees.

To carry out its objectives of promoting, encouraging, and educating in the arts, the museum offers an average of five major exhibitions annually. By far its most successful, in terms of attendance, publicity, and critical acclaim, was the Alexander Calder mobile-stabile sculpture show of the 1964 season. Its other successes have been exhibits devoted to Van Gogh, Francis Bacon, the Abstract Expressionists, Nicholas de Staël, and Kandinsky.

The Guggenheim museum began in 1937 as the Museum of Non-Objective Art, but changed its name and policies many years ago. In 1943, Frank Lloyd Wright was commissioned by Solomon R. Guggenheim, a mining magnate, to build this fascinating, unusual museum. Opposition came from the municipal Department of Buildings, whose opinions regarding its construction and locale were for many years at odds with Wright's. Sixteen years elapsed between the commission of the present Museum and its completion. Harry F. Guggenheim, nephew of the founder, and president of the Board of Trustees of the Solomon R. Guggenheim Foundation, said that the building was basically unchanged from the original plan, and that "its composition, its beauty, and its majesty are evident."

148 |

From the day it opened on October 21, 1959, the Wright building has proved a major attraction in New York, as much for the building as for the art it contains. It boasts nearly 800,000 visitors a year. One of the most controversial structures designed by the late architect, the

*The main floor dominated
by a large stabile by Calder.*

museum occupies almost an entire block fronting on Fifth Avenue.

Visitors take the elevator to the top landing and then walk down a circular half mile of sloping ramp until they hit bottom. "A museum," said Frank Lloyd Wright, "is an organic building where all is one great space on a single continuous floor." Progressing downward, the visitor views works of art seemingly floating in space. The art is set within cubicles or bays along the curved walls. Each cubicle is about large enough for two seven-foot-wide paintings. Except for the spiderweb

glass dome (ninety-five feet above the floor), there are no windows. There are almost no seats along the ramps, which are protected by a waist-high parapet.

Critical reaction to the $3-million museum has covered a wide range of opinion. The former director James Johnson Sweeney, who resigned in dissatisfaction over the museum, was faced with the problem of adapting an abstract architectural composition to function as an exhibition gallery. When the structure was unveiled, he simply said: "I have no statement to make at this time. I know you will understand." A newspaper editorial said it was a building "that should be put in a museum to show how mad the 20th century is." However, *Time* magazine claimed that the "great curved ramps provided the most dramatic setting abstract art has ever had." Emily Genauer writing in the *Herald Tribune* agreed that the structure was controversial, but stated that everyone said it "turned out to be the most beautiful building in America." John Canaday of *The New York Times* found it "a war between architecture and painting in which both come out badly maimed." See for yourself!

NATIONAL ACADEMY OF DESIGN
Address: 1083 5th Ave. (at 89th St.), New York, N.Y.
Phone: EN 9-4880

Days: Open weekdays, 1–5. Closed during the summer.
Admission: Up to $.50.

Subway: IRT Lexington Ave. to 86th St. station. Walk west to 5th Ave., north to building.
Bus: 5th Ave. or Madison Ave. bus to 89th St.
Auto: North on Park Ave. or Madison Ave. Limited street parking.

The National Academy of Design is in the Fifth Avenue town house that was originally built about 1900 for Archer Huntington, founder of the Hispanic Society. This building was given to the academy in 1940. A new building around the corner on 89th Street houses the School of Fine Arts of the National Academy. The style of the new building captures the spirit of the institution. | 151

The Academy's exhibition program consists of half a dozen group shows a year, among them the Fifty-second Annual Show of the Allied Artists of America, the One Hundredth Annual of the American Watercolor Society, the Twenty-fifth Annual of the Audubon

Inside the Guggenheim during the
Alexander Calder exhibition.

Artists, and the annuals of the New York Society of Women Artists or the National Association of Women Artists. This list, of course, should include the 142nd annual exhibition of the National Academy of Design.

The Academy was founded on November 8, 1825, with the intention of forming a group "that would be governed solely by artists for the development in this country of the highest standards in the arts." Members and associates were to be elected on the basis of "their standing as painters, sculptors, architects and workers in the graphic arts." The academy's founder and first president was Samuel Finley Breese Morse, artist, inventor, businessman, educator, and a leading citizen of New York. Of the thirty founding members, eleven are represented in the collections of the Metropolitan Museum of Art, and many famous and important architects, painters, sculptors, printmakers, and illustrators are currently members of the academy.

THE JEWISH MUSEUM

Address: 1109 5th Ave. (at 92nd St.), New York, N.Y.
Phone: 749-3770

Days: Open Sundays, 11–6; Mondays through Thursdays, 12–5; Fridays, 11–3. Closed Saturdays.
Admission: Adults $.50; children $.25; members free.

Subway: IRT Lexington Ave. to 96th St. station. Walk west to 5th Ave., south to museum.
Bus: 5th Ave. or Madison Ave. bus to 92nd St.
Auto: FDR (East River) Drive to 96th St. exit, east to 5th Ave., south 4 blocks. Limited street parking.

Gift Shop: Museum shop offers Jewish ceremonial objects, publications, and unique jewelry.

Membership: $18.00 up. Privileges include discounts on books, lounge and library privileges, admission to lectures, etc.

The Jewish Museum is the world's largest and most comprehensive repository of Jewish ceremonial art and other historical Judaica in the fine arts. It operates under the auspices of the Jewish Theological Seminary of America, one of the nation's foremost educational institutions. The collections and galleries are in the former home of Felix M.

The National Academy of Design.

Warburg. This French Renaissance landmark, built in 1908, was presented to the Jewish Theological Seminary by his widow, Mrs. Frieda Schiff Warburg. The adjoining modern wing, completed in 1962, is the Albert A. List building. The board of governors of the museum is under the chairmanship of Mrs. Albert A. List.

Museum activities are divided loosely into two categories: the permanent collections, which seek to illustrate the continuity between the accomplishments of the past and the present, and the changing-exhibition program that seeks to illustrate the temper and spirit of contemporary life.

The changing exhibitions are held on the first floor. On the other two floors are the permanent collections with their four categories: ceremonials used to mark the epochs of a lifetime, ceremonials associated

Silver Torah crowns at the Jewish Museum.

Visitors at the
Jewish Museum during
"The Lower East Side" exhibition.

with holidays, religious objects for the synagogue, and objects for the Jewish home. The Harry G. Friedman collection on the second floor shows Torah crowns, headpieces, breastplates, pointers, candelabra, Passover plates, amulets, Sabbath lamps, mezuzahs (door pieces), tefillin bags, Kiddush cups, embroidered linen Torah wrappers, scrolls; and silver ceremonial objects. The Benguiat Collection contains a | 155 Torah ark given to the synagogue of Urbino, Italy, in 1551. The ark, like the altar of a Christian church, is the focal point of the service, and contains the Torah, the scroll on which the Five Books of Moses are inscribed.

"Primary Structures" on display at the Jewish Museum.

A group of Italian ceremonial objects demonstrates a combination of finesse and beauty in the Italian decorative arts as applied to traditional Jewish ritual objects. In Europe in the Middle Ages many of these were fashioned for Jews by Christian artisans because Jews were not allowed to belong to the silversmiths' guilds.

The Samuel Friedenberg Collection of great Jewish portraits in metal is on the third floor. The medals and plaques commemorate Jewish notables. The entire collection is described in a comprehensive catalogue. This floor also has an interesting sixteenth-century synagogue wall of faience mosaic from Iraq, the only one from Persia in this country. The Philip and Lillian Leff Gallery contains an outstanding and extensive group of turret-form silver spice containers. A separate room houses the black-box sculpture "Homage to 6 Million" by Louise Nevelson. In 1966 the museum presented an immensely interesting and moving photographic exhibit called "The Lower East Side: Portal to American Life." Its depiction of the Lower East Side during the great wave of immigrants to this country proved so overwhelmingly popular that the exhibition was repeated.

The contemporary phase of the museum's activities was perhaps best exemplified by a group show of relatively unknown second-generation New York School artists. This exhibit, suggested by the art historian Meyer Schapiro, presented many artists who in a span of less than ten years have become leading contemporary artists.

More "Primary Structures."

The museum has shown the work of Max Ernst, Philip Guston, Jean Tinguely, Kenneth Noland, Larry Rivers, Jasper Johns, Robert Rauschenberg, and Ad Reinhardt. Some of these important one-man shows were arranged by the museum's former director, Alan R. Solomon, who also organized the group of works by American artists at the Venice Biennale of 1964, in which Rauschenberg was awarded the grand prize in painting. This was only the second time in the Biennale's long history that an American was honored. When Mr. Solomon left the museum, Sam Hunter became director.

Mr. Hunter summarized the museum's position in an article in *The New York Times:* "By force of cultural change, by intellectual sympathy and by choice, then, the Museum has been drawn into the orbit of contemporary art. . . . The Jewish Museum is in a position to give more weight and exhibition room to one-man shows by contemporary artists whose ultimate stature is still in dispute.

"The Jewish Museum can keep in touch with acknowledged major art of our time by showing phases of it that may have been neglected or summarily treated in previous retrospectives; it can also simply reacquaint us with an established artist's old virtues and qualities . . . the Museum can continue as before to make the new accessible even at the risk of appearing to be a trend-jumper. . . . I envision the Jewish Museum as a proving ground for viable new ideas in art and a hospitable forum for old ideas that have not outlived their time."

NATIONAL AUDUBON SOCIETY
Address: 1130 5th Ave. (at 94th St.), New York, N.Y.
Phone: EN 9-2100

Days: Open daily, 9–5.
Admission: Free.

Subway: IRT Lexington Ave. to 96th St. West to 5th Ave.
Bus: 5th Ave. or Madison Ave. bus to 94th St.
Auto: FDR (East River) Drive to 96th St. exit. West to 5th Ave.
Limited street parking.

158 | *Membership:* Adults $8.50, Family $12.50, call for Junior Members' fees.

In the beautiful building of the Audubon Society there is no major exhibition, but there are some displays in the sales room off the entrance

National Audubon Society.

hall. For sale are bird cages and bird houses. Audubon bird prints, the definitive "Birds of America" of Audubon, greeting cards, ashtrays, ceramic tiles with bird motifs, books on nature study for children and adults, and recordings of bird songs.

Built in 1915 by the architectural firm of Delano & Aldrich, the four-story red-brick Federal Eclectic mansion has a black iron peacock decorating the front doorway. The Audubon Society bought the property in 1952. The New York Community Trust designated the building a landmark in 1964.

The National Audubon Society, founded in 1905, ranks among the oldest, largest, and most important forces of conservation in North America. It is supported privately by membership dues, contributions, and bequests. It receives no government funds. Audubon Junior Clubs, which have enrolled nearly eleven million children, are sponsored by the society, which believes that "constructive conservation legislation requires an informed public."

Audubon Camps for adults eighteen to eighty are in Maine, Connecticut, Wisconsin, and Wyoming. A film-lecture program features the complex natural wildlife and plant-life stories told by naturalists and photographers in 225 communities throughout North America.

At Audubon sanctuaries wardens patrol over a million acres of land and water to furnish protection to great concentrations of nesting, roosting, and feeding birds. The society maintains an important field wildlife research program, and issues research reports.

The official publication, *Audubon Magazine,* is an illustrated bimonthly in its sixty-fifth year. It contains authoritative articles on birds, mammals, insects, plants, marine life, pesticides, biological controls, conservation, nature centers, camps, and sanctuaries. The society also publishes field notes, consevation guides, nature bulletins, nature charts, and maintains a public information center. The library on the second floor has 18,000 books, pamphlets, and ornithological magazines for reference use and is open to the public.

MUSEUM OF THE CITY OF NEW YORK

Address: 5th Ave., between 103rd and 104th Sts., New York, N.Y.
Phone: LE 4-1672

Days: Weekdays, 10–5; Sundays and holidays, 1–5. Closed Mondays, and on Christmas. When a legal holiday falls on a Monday, the museum is open.
Admission: Free.

Subway: IRT Lexington Ave. to 103rd St. station. Walk west to 5th Ave.
Bus: 5th Ave. or Madison Ave. bus to 104th St.
Auto: FDR (East River) Drive to 96th St. exit. West to Madison Ave., north to 103rd St. Limited street parking.

Gift Shop: Exceptionally well-stocked shop to left of lobby entrance sells books on New York, Delft miniatures, pewterware, toy reproductions of antique autos, souvenirs, etc.

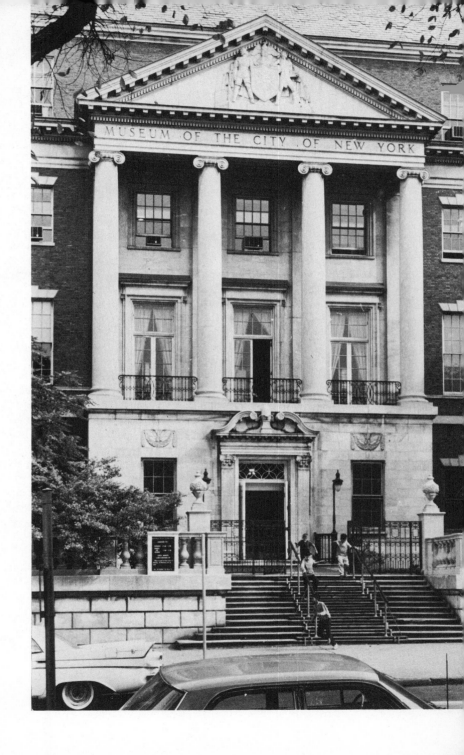

Membership: Annual membership $10.00 up. Members receive invitations to special events, discounts, and Calendar of Events.

Special Events: Concerts (for adults) Sundays at 3 from October to May. "Please Touch" demonstrations on alternate Saturdays, 10:30 and 11:30, October through May. Admission $.50. Puppet shows Saturdays at 1:30. Adults $1.00, children $.50 during school year. Also, puppet workshops for children.

Tours: Walking tours of New York City, alternate Sundays at 2:30, April to October. $2.50 fee; museum members, $1.50.

Dioramas of old New York, unique toys, costumes, fire engines, trolley cars, and clipper ships have attracted generations of city children to the Museum of the City of New York. The museum visually re-creates history so as to define our cultural heritage and describe, particularly for children, the story of New York City.

For an adult, the best place to start is on the fifth floor, with the Rockefeller rooms. A teen-ager might begin on the second floor, with the marine collection. Young children would start in the basement, where the water fountain and the fire engines are. The red-paneled Fire-Fighting Gallery has two life-size pumpers and a collection of miniature scale models of fire-fighting equipment, notably the first aerial ladder and a hose carriage. Old prints depict some of New York's early fires. The popular 1858 Currier & Ives print of the American fireman, "The Perfection of Graceful and Vigorous Manhood," is here. Much of this material duplicates the collection in the Fire Department Museum on Duane Street.

"Punch's Progress, Heroes of the Puppet Stage," interprets the evolution of Punch and Judy puppets, particularly those made by the master magician Harry Houdini. A puppet theatre stands next to this display. From early hand puppets to the current rod puppets used on television, the figures have grown significantly larger. For example, the Bread and Puppet Theater, a European group located in the Bowery, and not represented in this collection, uses puppets that are two stories high. The basement's miscellany is rounded off by a chronology of baseball from 1700 to 1950, with a dozen autographed baseballs and a panorama of Yankee Stadium, Ebbetts Field, and the Polo Grounds. The last two, of course, belong to history.

By taking the elevator to the fifth floor, one finds two rooms from a John D. Rockefeller house that stood at 4 West 54th Street. Rockefeller bought the house in 1884, about twenty-five years after it was built. Both the dressing room and bedroom were inspired by 1880 designs of the English architect Charles L. Eastlake. Satinwood with rosewood woodwork is inlaid with mother-of-pearl and intricate carvings. The plush elegance of the rooms epitomizes the grandeur of Victorian taste. The 54th Street house was demolished in 1938; the site is now occupied by the garden of the Museum of Modern Art. (Another roomful of furniture from the same house is on view in the Brooklyn Museum.)

On the fourth floor are administrative offices, study rooms, a print section, and the theatre and music collections, all of which can be seen by appointment. The third floor has the most diverse collection of doll-houses and toys available in any museum. Enchanting six-room minia-ture reproductions of complete scale-model houses, toy theatres, paper dolls, zoos, trolley cars, trains, pewter tea sets, animal farms, teddy bears, penny mechanical banks, iron coal stoves, complete kitchens,

A selection of Victorian furniture.

| 163

and hobbyhorses offer children entertainment on a rainy afternoon.

About thirty-five dolls from the Sophia McDonald Collection provide excellent examples, some extremely rare, of almost every type of doll made from the late-eighteenth to the mid-nineteenth century. "Mehitabel Hodges," one of the oldest known imported dolls in America, was brought here from France in 1724.

"The History and Progress of Communications in New York" is dramatically presented by a series of dioramas showing the overland mail service, use of visual signals, Morse laying the submarine cable,

*Ship's figurehead of
Andrew Jackson from
the frigate "Constitution," 1812.*

the first stock ticker, telephone, radio, and the effects of the blizzard of
'88. In front of each little boxlike theatre that houses a diorama, a
ladder enables children to step up to see.

The third-floor corridor contains an early nineteenth-century
Duncan Phyfe drawing room. All the chairs, card table, sewing table,
and other pieces here were made in his workshop from 1795 to 1847,
and sold from his warehouse and store at 168 Fulton Street.

A collection of retail storefronts is re-created in the Harry T. Peters
Gallery. Visitors can walk behind the storefronts of such retail land-
marks as Belters Victorian Furniture, 547 Broadway; Kate Green
Toys, 916 Broadway; Gale & Willis Silverware, 447 Broome Street;
and so on, and look at products that were once for sale as common
objects but have now achieved the status of antiques and works of art.

On the second floor the museum's marine collection relates the mari-
time development of the city, from its Dutch trading-post days to the
present. (These scale models and exhibits complement the extensive
collection in the Marine Museum of the Seamen's Institute on Coenties
Slip.) One diorama shows the Florentine navigator Giovanni da Verrazano startling the Indians as he sails into New York harbor in 1524.
The diorama of the South Street waterfront during the clipper-ship
era is so realistic that it is outdone only by the new forced-perspective
technique used in a shipbuilding diorama that creates a fantastic illu-
sion of depth, and offers a 360-degree view of Victorian New York.
The model was built by Arthur Henning, Inc. Figureheads, scale
models of tugs, cutters, and ferries generate the excitement and adven-
ture that have always been part of the great harbor. The second floor
also has a gallery devoted to the history and development of Wall
Street.

The remaining gallery on the second floor contains six large alcoves
of authentic room settings, some with costumed mannequins. There are
an 1830 drawing room, from 7 Bowling Green; a 1760 English Colonial interior, from 29 Cherry Street; a 1906 drawing room, from
32 Park Avenue; and a Victorian drawing room, from 1 Pierrepont
Street. The periods from 1690 to 1740 are also represented.

A number of fine American portraits hang on the first floor. In the
Altman Foundation Gallery is a fascinating display of maps, prints,
and views of early New York that trace the city's progress from 1800. | 165

The newly installed Davies Gallery on the first floor displays ship
models of the *Half Moon* and *Dauphine*. Other exhibits relate to the
period of Dutch settlement, as well as to the background of European
events that led to the age of exploration and colonization. A diorama

A bedroom from the Rockefeller house.

of Fort Amsterdam gives a 360-degree forced-perspective view of the skyline as it looked in 1660.

In addition to permanent and temporary exhibits, the museum conducts Sunday Walking Tours of every historical section of New York, from the Battery to Brooklyn. Under the expert direction of the historian Henry Hope Reed, Jr., these popular two-hour excursions offer a unique opportunity to explore New York's history and architecture. Special tours are also conducted by Spanish-speaking guides.

The museum's "Please Touch" exhibits are for children aged six to thirteen. They can handle seventeenth- and eighteenth-century household objects. This is but one of many features the museum offers to thousands of schoolchildren who visit each year.

The Dazian Library, a collection of material on the visual arts of the stage, is open to students, historians, and designers. The museum library has a collection of New York City guidebooks dating from 1807, histories, biographies, and city directories. The first directory was compiled in 1786.

When the Museum of the City of New York first opened, on July 31, 1923, it was in Gracie Mansion in Carl Schurz Park, at 88th Street and the East River. In January, 1932, the museum moved into its present Georgian building, which was designed by Joseph H. Freedlander. The average annual attendance is about 220,000. The museum is a non-profit organization operated by an independent Board of Trustees. The city's contribution toward the annual cost of operating the museum is so minimal that the principal funds must come from membership dues, gifts, bequests, and special fund-raising events.

The museum plans a program of re-orienting many of its collections of decorative arts as related to material on the political and economic growth of the city. New exhibits will present the history of the city in chronological order; each period will be illustrated with appropriate costumes, furniture, portraits, and household items.

In outlining the extensive improvement program, the museum's director, Ralph Miller, indicates that in the past the educational effectiveness of the museum has been estimated by the number of people who viewed the collections; but now "quantity in attendance is no longer an adequate gauge. . . . The aim is to surround the visitor with history by giving him the total picture of each era—economic, political and social—leading him through in a lovely, logical progression."

THE NEW-YORK HISTORICAL SOCIETY
Address: Central Park West at 77th St., New York, N.Y.
Phone: TR 3-3400

Days: Museum open daily, except Mondays, 1–5; Saturdays, 10–5. Library open daily, except Sundays, 10–5; holidays, 1–5. Closed on major holidays.
Admission: Free.

Subway: IND 8th Ave. to 81st St. station. Walk south to museum.
Bus: 8th Ave. and Central Park West buses to 77th St.
Auto: West Side Highway to 79th St. exit, east to Central Park West. | 167
Limited street parking.

Gift Shop: Publications of the society, postcards for sale.

Membership: Annual fee $10.00.

The New-York Historical Society.

Special Events: Free films, concerts for children and adults, special
school programs, guided tours for groups. Calendar of Events,
printed three times a year and available at Information Desk, lists
complete activities.

The New-York Historical Society building contains fine portraits, historic prints, rare maps, handmade furniture, toys, and household furnishings—all of which are not only beautiful but also represent the
roots from which many New Yorkers grew.

The New-York Historical Society, founded by John Pintard and ten
leading citizens, occupied the first City Hall from 1804 until 1809. For
about thirty years the society was always either in or close to City Hall.

Early New York City milestones.

In 1837 it moved uptown to 659 Broadway, into the Stuyvesant Institute, and then to the northeast corner of Washington Square East, where the Main building of New York University is now. For the next fifty years, from 1857, the society was at 170 Second Avenue, at 11th Street. After seven moves, it settled on Central Park West in 1908.

The collections of the society should be seen by everyone interested in this city. As the curator, Richard J. Koke, has said, "The items which have come to the Society in 160 years of collecting Americana are outstanding." Quality, not quantity, has been the yardstick for acquisition.

As you enter the building, the first gallery is devoted to John James Audubon's "Birds of America." A number of the original drawings from that extraordinary volume hang in the gallery. Audubon drew 1,065 life-sized bird portraits representing 489 species found in North America. He published the double Elephant Folio engravings, all hand colored and drawn from nature, after considerable effort to solicit a subscription fund to cover its expense. In 1838, approximately 200

One of the main galleries showing a wooden water main (right foreground).

volumes were published, priced at $1,000 each. The New-York Historical Society has four volumes. The gallery was recently refurbished to house this priceless collection, and the prints are rotated frequently.

The American Silver Gallery is particularly rich in the works of early New York silversmiths, such as Benjamin Wynkoop, who worked from 1690; Thauvet Besley (1727), Myer Myers (1745), Daniel Christian Fueter (1754), William G. Forbes (1773), and Garret Eoff (1806). (The Brooklyn Museum has some samples of the work of Jacob Boelen and Jacobus van der Spiegel, who worked in New York before 1750. Other major collections of American silver are in the Museum of the City of New York and the Metropolitan.)

The period covered here ranges from about 1730 to 1850. Tankards, porringers, canns, salvers, toasting forks, sugar tongs, candle snuffers, nutmeg graters, snuffboxes, winetasters, tea caddies, toddy pots, salt-cellars, and some commemorative silver pieces are on display.

Silver was introduced to America with the arrival in 1635 of Richard Storer from England. As the colonies prospered, the use of silver increased, but most of it was produced in order to celebrate domestic events.

On the first floor are views of New York from 1679 to 1900. There is a wealth of maps, drawings, and colored lithographs of general views, churches, theatres, hotels, the harbor and waterfront, street scenes, and bridges. An auditorium is in the center of the first floor, and hallways around it display views of the Hudson River.

In the basement of the museum is the Fahnestock carriage collection of Brewster and Company coaches of the 1900's—Stanhope Gig, Park Drag, Tandem Cart, Panel Book Victoria, road coaches, and caleches. They are accompanied by a collection of New York City milestones, resembling fat tombstones, which marked the miles from City Hall to Kingsbridge, a distance of fourteen stones, and were important features of the early highway system. Oftentimes stagecoach inns were located at the milestones. The first group of stones was made in 1769 by George Lindsay.

A Volunteer Firemen's section is devoted to scale models and full-sized ancient equipment. This represents the third major collection of fire-fighting archives in the city. Special emphasis here is on prints and documentation of the conflagration of December 16, 1838, which wiped out a staggering portion of lower Manhattan in the Water Street, Front Street, Coenties Slip area.

On the second floor are the research library and De Peyster gallery. The Katherine Prentis Murphy collections display early American wooden and mechanical toys, such as carved wooden horses, beaded doll furniture, toy soldiers, Noah's ark with three hundred animals, squeak toys, pottery banks, and whistles and jackstraws. Noteworthy is a large group of hand-carved animals by Wilhelm Schimmel, an itinerant Pennsylvania woodcarver who made toys in exchange for room and board.

To the right are galleries illustrating New York under Dutch rule. An old New York map pinpoints the locations of the Indian tribes that inhabited Manhattan. Outstanding in this collection are examples of the Duke of York laws of 1665; a remarkable sepia painting, dated

Cigar store Indians.

1679, of a Dutch cottage on Beaver Street; Peter Stuyvesant's Bible of 1637, and William Bradford's cracked tombstone. A copy of the tombstone is now in Trinity Churchyard.

The major exhibition in the center gallery of the Revolutionary and Federal periods is divided into historic sections dating from 1763 to 1800, and covers the struggle for the Hudson River, New York as a Federal City, the Presidency, Revolutionary battles, and British occupation and evacuation. The famous portrait of George Washington by Gilbert Stuart is here.

On the left are galleries with New York stoneware jugs, Rockingham pottery, American glass, earthenware, Worcester porcelain, green glazed pottery, Delftware salt-glaze ware, and Whieldon ware. The J. Insley Blair Collection of Old Blue English Staffordshire ware, depicting historical scenes of New York and New England, is one of the finest collections of this china in the country.

The completely furnished eighteen-century parlor, bedroom, and seventeenth-century dining room reconstructed in this gallery form part of the Prentis Collection of Colonial New England. The collection also contains a number of printed cotton kerchiefs and textiles that commemorate historical events and personalities. The earliest, immortalizing George Washington, were printed in England and France in the 1800's.

In the third-floor galleries and corridors are folk art paintings of the highest quality, American pewter, lighting devices, household utensils, cigar-store wooden Indians, painted boxes, signs and weathervanes, paintings on glass, old advertisements and posters. There is a map

Early American pottery and furniture.

Three paintings from "The Course of Empire"
series by Thomas Cole.

room, as well as a brand-new gallery for Early American military
weapons, equipment ranging from flintlocks of Colonial days to
weapons of the late nineteenth century. A group of sixty-seven figurines, dressed in costumes from 1610 to 1946, can also be found on
this floor.

At the top of the stairs on the fourth floor is a marble sculpture by
Thomas Crawford, who also did the colossal figures surmounting the
dome of the United States Capitol. The title of this piece is "The
Dying Chief Contemplating the Progress of Civilization."

The fourth-floor galleries are predominantly used for showing the
paintings of prominent individuals, including Dutch New York portraits, Colonial New York portraits, presidents and statesmen, promi-
174 | nent men in the history of the Revolution, American artists and
authors, late-eighteenth-century and nineteenth-century American
landscape and genre painting. There is, oddly, one gallery devoted to
Italian Renaissance painting.

There are a number of extremely fine paintings in these galleries,

Portraits of American historical figures.

particularly in the presidential and landscape groups, where there are works by Asher B. Durand, Thomas Sully, Rembrandt Peale, Samuel F. B. Morse, John Trumbull, and Thomas Cole. Some of the painters themselves are the subjects of paintings in the section on artists. The recently acquired self-portrait of Thomas Cole, for example, is the only one known to exist. It complements the Society's renowned series of four paintings by Cole called "The Course of Empire," which hang nearby.

The American furniture collection of the seventeenth, eighteenth, and nineteenth centuries features, in chronological order, examples

| 175

of New England, Hudson River Valley, Pennsylvania, and New York City cabinetwork. An unusual wardrobe by Thomas Burling of New York City, about 1790, is one of the very rare labeled pieces. There are some pieces of Victorian furniture carved by John Henry Belter. Any student or scholar of American or New York history would find these paintings and household furnishings an invaluable source of knowledge.

For New York City schoolchildren, as well as adults, the Society offers an extensive educational program that includes special school programs, a concert series, motion pictures, filmstrips, publications, guided tours, high-school loan exhibitions, story hours, puppet shows, and folk music. The Society is a privately endowed institution, and receives no financial support from the city. Its annual attendance is now about 96,000.

THE AMERICAN MUSEUM OF NATURAL HISTORY
Address: Central Park West at 79th St., New York, N.Y.
Phone: TR 3-1300

Days: Open weekdays, 10–5; Sundays and holidays, 1–5.
Admission: Free.

Subway: IND 8th Ave. to 81st St. station.
Bus: (1) 79th St. crosstown bus connects with East Side subways.
(2) 8th Ave. or Columbus Ave. bus to 79th St.
Auto: West Side Highway to 79th St. exit, east to Central Park West. Parking lot adjacent to Planetarium on West 81st St. Open Sundays and holidays, 12:30–6:30; Monday through Saturday, 9:30–6:30. Fee is $1.00 for private cars, $2.00 for buses. Metered street parking behind museum.

Restaurant: Cafeteria in lower level of Roosevelt Memorial Building serves hot meals and snacks. No box lunches permitted. Open weekdays, 11:30–4:30, Sundays and holidays, 1–4:30.

Gift Shop: Museum Shop offers museum reproductions, nature records, native handicrafts, mineral and shell specimens, color slides, prints and books. Sales area near cafeteria features merchandise especially for children, such as nature hobby kits, souvenirs.

Special Events: Free Calendar of Events, published monthly September

The American Museum of Natural History.

to June mailed free of charge within the metropolitan area. Museum lectures, field trips, and tours for adults at nominal cost. Free films and lectures weekdays as announced. Free films for children and family groups on Saturday.

Membership: Annual membership is $5.00. Benefits include 10 issues of *Natural History Magazine,* 10% book discount, use of Members' Room, Calendar of Events. More expensive annual memberships, $15.00 and up, have additional benefits such as admission to Planetarium, and invitations to special lectures.

Library: For research only, Monday to Friday, 10–4. Closed Saturday, Sunday, and holidays.

Tours: Acoustiguide taped tours last approximately one hour, cost $.50 for one earphone, $.75 for two. Available on second floor of Roosevelt Memorial Building. Guide service for groups, weekdays only, for nominal fee. Write Department of Education for arrangements.

Children's Facilities: Natural Science Center for Young People. School study aids available to teachers. See Calendar of Events for other children's activities.

The American Museum of Natural History, the largest institution in the world devoted to the natural sciences, is directly across Central Park from that other mammoth institution, the Metropolitan Museum of Art. The American Museum was originally housed in the Arsenal building in Central Park along Fifth Avenue. Its physical plant now occupies three city blocks. The section facing West 77th Street, in Romanesque Revival style with segmented arches and imposing turrets, makes it obvious that this is a museum in the classic sense. This great museum receives over 2,000,000 visitors annually.

The section facing Central Park West was designed by the architect John Russell Pope in 1936 as a memorial to Theodore Roosevelt. The colossal scale of the main entrance is particularly evident from the inside. Pope's Colonnade Court can be seen at the Frick Collection.

The American Museum has approximately fifty-eight exhibition areas, each of which constitutes a small-size museum. The twenty-three acres of floor space include scientific and educational offices, laboratories, libraries, photography departments, restoration workshops, and storage areas, that contain tens of millions of zoological, geological, anthropological, and botanical specimens for use by scientists, students, and scholars from all over the world. The museum also maintains field stations on Long Island, in Florida, Arizona, and the Bahamas. Its expeditions are always in progress.

The idea of the museum was conceived by Professor Albert Smith Bickmore, a naturalist who studied at Harvard. In 1865 he sailed for the Spice Islands, and in three years traveled 40,000 miles throughout the East Indies, Asia, and Europe, collecting birds, shells, and other specimens. The museum was formally established in 1869, and the two guiding principles that give meaning and order to this vast institution are the evolution of life and the interdependence of all living things, including man.

The museum's scientific departments include: Animal Behavior, Anthropology, Astronomy, Entomology, Fossil Invertebrates, Herpetology, Ichthyology, Living Invertebrates, Mammalogy, Micropaleontology, Mineralogy, Ornithology, and Vertebrate Paleontology. The education section includes the departments of Exhibitions and Graphic Arts, the Library, Scientific Publications, and *Natural History Magazine*. The educational program includes evening lectures, field walks

Totempoles made by American Indians of the Northwest Coast.

| 179

in natural science, museum tours, scientific-society meetings, and programs for young people conducted in the Natural Science Center. These programs highlight the wildlife of the metropolitan region, and present demonstrations of live animals. The American Museum also has courses for teachers in the social and natural sciences, and conducts a nursing education program.

Exhibits of the museum's collections are divided into the following categories: Astronomy, Birds, Invertebrates, Mammals, Man, Man's Environment, Minerals, Prehistoric Life, and Reptiles. The museum distributes a floor plan that shows the location of exhibits on all four floors. It was recently announced that the museum would open eight new exhibit halls by 1969 as part of the celebration of the 100th anniversary of the founding of the museum. These new halls will be called Ocean Life (which will feature a 91-foot model of a blue whale), Man in Africa, Indians of the Plains, the Biology of Invertebrates, the Biology of Fishes, Earth History, Mexico and Central America, and People of the Pacific.

*Crossection of
a giant Sequoia.*

*A peregrine falcon brings food to
its young on the New Jersey Palisades.*

"Biology of Birds" shows how birds originated, the kinds of birds
that exist, those that are extinct, how birds fly, migrate, court, and
breed. Three skeletons of giant flightless birds are shown—the ostrich,
moa, and the Diatryma, a huge billed bird, dug up in Wyoming, that
lived 50 million years ago.

"Oceanic Birds" were brought to the museum by the Whitney South
Sea expedition (1920 to 1940), which was unique both in its duration and in the geographic area covered. Over 250 kinds of birds
previously unknown to science were collected. Thorough study of the
material brought back broadened concepts in the fields of evolution
and distribution of life. This hall, showing about eighteen bird groups
in various oceanic settings, was presented to the museum, together
with a unique collection of 280,000 bird specimens acquired over a | 181
lifetime by Lord Rothschild, by Mrs. Harry Payne Whitney.

"Birds of the World" presents twelve realistic settings showing the
differences in bird life from continent to continent. "North American
Birds" in the Frank M. Chapman Memorial Hall shows 160 species

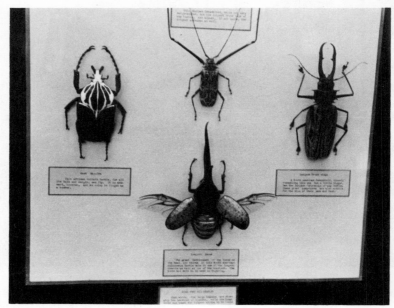

Giant beetles.

of birds in settings approximating their natural habitat. Upland game birds, common loons, desert birds, marsh birds, whooping cranes, California condors, the bald eagle, and peregrine falcon are all placed in realistic settings. The fascination and beauty of these life-size dioramas are due to the splendid background mural paintings of Fred Scherer, Raymond de Lucia, Matthew Kallmenoff, and Richard Kane, working with George E. Petersen, the Preparation Supervisor. Their search for new exhibit techniques never ends. Specialists are now studying a method of freeze-drying specimens that could revolutionize modern taxidermy.

"The Biology of Invertebrates" covers the origin and the structure of life. When this gallery is finished, it will illustrate some universal biological themes by means of exhibits of the animal species lacking backbones. The continuity and adaptability of life, as well as its interdependence, will be illustrated.

Insects are arranged with special reference to those in New York. Their origin, structure, habits, variations, and the ways in which they benefit man are shown, as well as means of identifying them. There are thousands of classic pinned-butterfly displays. A spider zoo in a sealed case contains tarantulas, black widows, and scorpions. There are also enlarged wax models of mosquitoes and other insects, and a section devoted to the silkworm.

The visitor will soon see that the "Reptiles" section is one of the most popular but least modern exhibitions in the museum. The presentation of these wide-ranging exhibits of reptiles, illustrate their many diversities in size, form, habit, and modes of reproduction.

"Ice Age Mammals" are depicted in this gallery, with striking examples of the evolution of the proboscideans, including the long-jawed, shovel-jawed, beak-jawed, and flat-toothed mastodons, and on to the southern hairless mammoths, northern woolly mammoths, and elephants of Africa and India. There are also several giant sloths from the famous La Brea tar pits in Los Angeles (now the site of the Los Angeles County Museum).

Skeletons of men and apes.

| 183

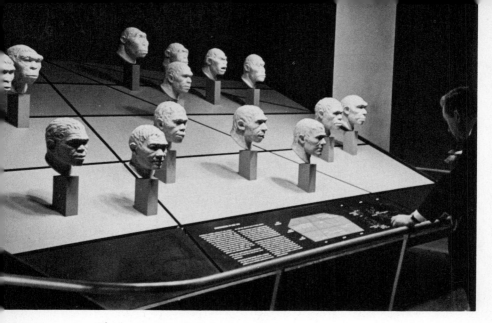

The forerunners of modern man.

"Early Mammals" shows the origin, spread, isolation, and extinction of these Mesonychids, Oxyaenids, and Hyaenodonts. A modern wall display explains how fossils are buried and preserved, then collected, cleaned, prepared, restored, identified, and finally classified by period.

"Late Mammals of the Cenozoic Period," the even-toed and odd-toed hoofed mammals, outlines the evolution of the horse, the camel, rhino, and antelope.

"The Late Dinosaurs" contains the most comprehensive display of Cretaceous dinosaur skeletons in existence. Tyrannosaurus Rex, Triceratops, and Trachodonts are grouped in the center island of the gallery. These monsters once existed in the general region of Montana, and were among the last dinosaurs to live on earth. Other examples of dinosaurs to be found here are the horned, armored, aquatic duck-billed, dome-headed dinosaurs, and flying reptiles.

"Early Dinosaurs" is by far the most popular exhibit in the museum. The center island has three great monsters of the Jurassic period: the 67-foot Brontosaurus, the dagger-jawed Allosaurus, and the spiked-tailed Stegosaurus, all of which roamed the Far West about 140 million years ago. At the base of the display are two pairs of Brontosaurus footprints collected in Texas. Another particularly interesting exhibit is the fossil skeleton of a dinosaur found by a geology class from Columbia University in 1910 in the Palisades near the site of the George Washington Bridge. This is appropriately labeled Fort Lee Phytosaur, Clepsysaurus Manhattanensis. The history of fossil fishes is to be found at the far end of the gallery.

"The Biology of Mammals" has as its star attraction the huge 76-foot model of a sulphur-bottom whale, hung by wires directly in the center pit of the gallery. The exhibit illustrates distinctive mammal characteristics, the various evolutionary groups and families, and their geologic history. The African lion, first specimen in this collection of mammals, was purchased in Paris in 1869, and is an example of the best taxidermy of the period. His tail is sewn on.

The "Primates" section is one of those recently reinstalled. The distinctive chracteristics and relationship of the different groups of primates are shown, including the tiny tree shrews, the lemurs, tarsiers, spider monkeys, howlers, bearded sakis, gorillas, apes, chimpanzees, and man. About 185 of the 5,500 living species of mammals are primates. Charts outline the development of hands, feet, vision, the senses, and reproduction.

In the Hall of the Dinosaurs.

"African Mammals" are on view in twenty-eight alcoves on two floors of the Carl Akeley Memorial Hall. A balcony offers a fine view of the group of elephants that are mounted in the center of the lower floor. Akeley was a renowned sculptor, taxidermist, conservationist, and inventor who survived incredible adventures. He was once pinned under an elephant, and at another time he strangled a wounded leopard when he ran out of ammunition. He succumbed to fever and exhaustion on his Belgian Congo expedition in 1926 and is buried on the slopes of Mount Mikeno, high in his beloved gorilla country. These beautifully displayed mammals are the results of his expeditions.

Akeley never lived to see the African Plains displays, among the most popular and impressive exhibits in the museum, for these exhibits are startling in their reality. The animals are shown in a complete environment of rocks, bushes, vegetation, insects, trees, water, and background murals of the terrain. One dramatic scene shows hyenas, jackals, and vultures attacking a zebra. In another, white rhinos are being stalled off at a water hole by a porcupine. Beautiful impalas graze in the open fields, mandrills inhabit the rain forest, and wart hogs fix their eyes on ostrich eggs hatching under the protection of the frightened parents.

"North American Mammals," another group of dramatic habitats, displays game and fur-bearing species—bison, white sheep, coyotes, mountain lions—in environmental settings, including Mount McKinley, the Grand Canyon, and the Great Smokies.

Materials for "South Asiatic Mammals" were collected in 1922 on expeditions into India, Burma, and Siam by Arthur S. Vernay and Colonel J. C. Faunthrope. In this gallery's realistic settings are the most complete exhibit of larger South Asiatic mammals in existence, including Indian antelopes, gaurs, leopards, sambars, sloth bear, chevrotains, bantings, and other rare animals. A pair of Indian elephants stand in the center of the gallery.

"Men of Montaña," the story of life in the Peruvian rain forest, is complete with warbling, croaking, sound effects of bird calls that, in the subdued illumination, lend an atmosphere appropriate to the exhibits of tribes of primitive Amazon Indians. The exhibits compare the cultures of the Montaña Indians, those of the Amazon basin, and of the Andean people by showing how they farm, fight, fish, hunt, and make artworks. Articles of recreation, adornment, and ceremonial life are included. Among these Indians are the headhunting Jivaro of Ecuador (see Museum of the American Indian). The mountainous terrain, deep jungles, and swift rivers not only keep the area inaccessible but also separate the various tribes in the rain forest, so that each

Zebras of the African plains.

one maintains a cultural entity. Though the Upper Amazon region is a rich source of rubber, cocaine, quinine, oil, and hardwood, it is still relatively unknown and unexplored by scientists and has not appeared in the literature of exotic vacation tours.

"The Eskimo Gallery" in the horseshoe around the auditorium depicts the culture of tribes in Canada, Alaska, and Greenland. "Indians of the Northwest Coast" illustrates the domestic and cultural mores of the Kwakiutl Indians of Vancouver, with a scale model showing an entire village. A 64-foot seagoing war canoe of the Haida tribe is displayed in the center of the 77th Street foyer, one of the main entrances of the museum.

The "Hall of the Indians of the Plains" concentrates on the culture of the twenty-five tribes that roamed the plains from the Mississippi to the Rockies and from Texas to Canada until the last quarter of the nineteenth century. The exhibit features six life-sized figures in costumes of dressed skin, heavily decorated with beadwork and the quills of porcupines.

"The Biology of Man," a departure from the standard museum exhibits, presents the very latest in visual material that documents life by explaining human cells, endocrine regulation, digestion, growth, and the functions of sensory perception. Heads of Cro-Magnon Man, Peking Man, and other forerunners of *Homo sapiens* are displayed on a platform, showing the successive types that reflect the course of

A group of elephants in Akeley Hall.

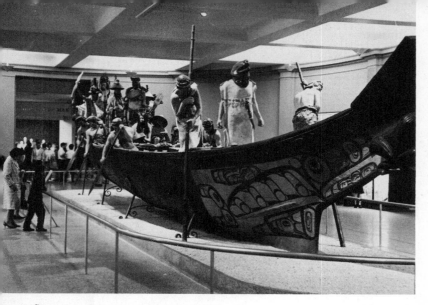

Sea-going war canoe from British Columbia.

human evolution. An unusual zoological wall chart in tile classifies man and his forebears.

The most startling section of the exhibit contains unique plastic specimens of the human fetus in about six stages of growth. This remarkable exhibit is accompanied by (plastic) specimens of lungs, the heart, intestines, and other internal organs. The human circulatory system is graphically presented by means of a life-size plastic sculpture of a woman that also may be lighted to show the functions of the human nervous system.

"Man and Nature" in the Felix M. Warburg Memorial Hall features landscape settings and exhibits relating human activities and the cycle of life in the soil. The Hall of North American Forests shows the diversity of communities in middle North America, the internal functions of our forests, and how man benefits from them. Life-size dioramas show huge cedar forests, the rain forests near Olympia, Washington, and others. There is a cross section of a giant Sequoia that was 330 feet tall, with a trunk circumference of ninety feet. In 1891, two men took thirteen days to cut the tree down. The section contains 1,342 annual rings, which indicates that the growth of the tree began in 550 A.D.

In the Hall of Ice Age Mammals.

"The Hall of Oil Geology" tells the story of oil, its formation by plants and animals during millions of years of the earth's history, the geological methods used to find it, and methods for extracting it, as well as other exhibits related to the long transition from the Age of Coal to the Age of Petroleum.

"The Evelyn Miles Keller Memorial Shell Exhibit" shows the six classes of mollusks from all over the world. This interesting seashell collection, in addition to showing shells as objects of aesthetic beauty, illustrates how they have been used by man for food, utensils, ornaments, money, implements, medicine, and even as a source for dye.

The enormous and overwhelming "Gem Collection" donated by J.

A gorilla in his natural habitat.

Pierpont Morgan defines minerals, rocks, and gems, and divides the collection into silicates, carbonates, oxides, haloids and so forth, arranged in systematic table and wall cases. Over 90 percent of all known minerals are contained here.

In 1964 a bizarre and spectacular jewel robbery drew attention to this gallery, and nowadays the hall is usually jammed on weekends with visitors who crowd around the black steel cases to see the recovered gems: the light-blue Star of India (563 carats), the world's largest star sapphire, which is the size of a golf ball; the Delong Star Ruby (100 carats), considered the most perfect star ruby in existence; and the purplish-blue Midnight Star Sapphire (116 carats), which is 1½ inches in diameter. These three stones, among the twenty-four that figured in the great theft, now appear on a colored picture post card. Meanwhile, the entire gallery has been rigged with an improved alarm system, and anyone with particularly sensitive ears can pick up the high-frequency pitch of the detection devices.

After the robbery, Dr. James A. Oliver, director of the museum, said emphatically that security was poor because the museum is understaffed. He said that officers of the museum had been pleading with City Hall for ten years to increase the staff. Since the robbery the number of guards has been increased, but the wide publicity has done little to awaken New York City to the pathetic condition of its cultural archives, historic houses, museums, libraries, and many public parks where these institutions are situated.

THE AMERICAN MUSEUM–HAYDEN PLANETARIUM

Address: Central Park West at 81st St., New York, N.Y.
Phone: TR 3-1300

Days: Shows every day of the year. Schedule as follows:
Saturday   11 A.M., 1, 2, 3, 4, 5, and 7:30 P.M.
Sunday   1, 2, 3, 4, 5, and 7:30 P.M.
Weekdays   2, 3:30, and 7:30 P.M. (no 7:30 show on Mondays)
Holidays   Call TR 3-8828 for schedule.
Special summer schedule during July, August, and September.
Admission: Matinees, adults, $1.20; children $.60. Evenings, adults $1.50; children $.75. Children under 5 not admitted.

Subway: IND 8th Ave. to 81st St. station.
Bus: (1) 79th St. crosstown bus connects with East Side subways.
(2) 8th Ave. or Columbus Ave. bus to 81st St.

Auto: West Side Highway to 79th St. exit. Parking lot adjacent to Planetarium on West 81st St. Open Sundays and holidays, 12:30–6:30; Monday through Saturday, 9:30–6:30. Fee is $1.00 for private cars, $2.00 for buses. Metered street parking behind museum.

Gift Shop: The Book Corner on the first floor sells publications on astronomy, space science, star-finders and charts, cards, prints, and souvenirs.

Lectures: Courses in the spring and fall for adults and children on astronomy, navigation, and meteorology.

There is a direct entrance from the American Museum of Natural History to the Hayden Planetarium, which occupies its own building facing a large open park on West 81st Street. The building, easily identified by its green dome, is one of ten planetariums in the United States. About 600,000 visitors come each year to visit the planetarium, which was made possible by a gift in 1937 of the philanthropist Charles Hayden. He believed that a planetarium should be a "place of interest and instruction . . . it should give a more lively and sincere appreciation of the magnitude of the universe . . . the belief that there must be a much greater power than man, responsible for the wonderful things occurring in the universe." As S. I. Gale, chief lecturer for twenty-two years, said after his six thousandth lecture on the day he retired, "There are no atheists at the eyepiece of a telescope."

The round building has two floors, both of which exhibit displays of compelling contemporary significance and interest. To the right of the main entrance is the Book Corner, a headquarters for technical books on astronomy, navigation, and meteorology, for celestial globes and paraphernalia for home and classroom use. A catalogue describes courses in astronomy and navigation for adults as well as for young people. On four mornings a week the program of the Planetarium is reserved for school classes.

Directly in the center of the first floor is a lecture theatre called the Hall of the Sun. Overhead, a Copernican planetarium, more than forty feet in diameter, shows the relative sizes and speeds of the planets and the satellites by means of globes revolving around a central sun. Corridors around the hall, all dimly illuminated, are lined with exhibits simulating outer space. A "black-light" tunnel of perpetual night, with large luminescent, color-activated murals puts the

A meteorite.

viewer in the shadowy mountains and craters of the lunar landscape. Other murals vividly detail solar eclipses, the planets, and galactic and spiral nebulae.

One remarkable exhibit shows the Ahnighito Meteorite, the largest on display anywhere. This great mass was dug up from the frozen wastelands of Greenland by Admiral Robert E. Peary in 1894. Twelve teams of horses were needed to haul the huge 34-ton meteorite from the docks. The Toledo Scale Company built a special platform scale for it. Visitors can stand on the scale and add their own weight to the 68,085 pounds already registered.

A set of scales on the second floor illustrates a person's weight on other planets. If you weigh 150 pounds on Earth, on Jupiter you would weigh 430 pounds; on Venus, 140 pounds; on Mars, 62 pounds; and on the Moon a mere 26 pounds. The major exhibit on the second floor is the IBM Astronomia, designed and developed by Gordon Ashby. The exhibition, arranged in chronologies of one hundred years, outlines the major achievements, developments, and theories in the science of astronomy from the year 1400.

The main lecture theatre, on the second floor, houses the huge Zeiss projector that showers the entirely perforated stainless-steel dome with millions of stars to create a perfect sky on a clear night.

The solar system and the miracles of the boundless universe, in perpetual, dramatic flux, are the stars of the show. It is truly a breathtaking experience to see the simulated sky fill with heavenly bodies and to hear the majestic music. For city dwellers this star-studded dome is a wonder that comes to life only in a planetarium or on a trip to the adjacent countryside. The lecture is delivered, live, by one of a staff of nine that operates the panel of forty knobs controlling the projector. The lecturer has over two thousand possible combinations at his command, and is thus virtually in command of the universe.

Various displays at the Hayden Planetarium.

RIVERSIDE MUSEUM

Address: 310 Riverside Drive (at 103rd Street), New York, N.Y.
Phone: UN 4-1700

Days: Open Tuesday through Sundays, 1–5. Closed holidays, July, and
August.
Admission: Free.

Subway: IRT Broadway-242nd St. train to 103rd St. station. Walk
west one block.
Bus: 5th Ave. (Riverside Drive) bus to 103rd St.
Auto: West Side Highway to 96th St. exit; then north to Riverside
Drive. Ample street parking.

Special Events: Concert series, other programs as announced.
The Riverside Museum, a unit of the Master Institute of United Arts,
Inc., takes up the lower floors of a twenty-nine-story residential apartment hotel built during the real-estate boom of the late twenties,
Although the building employs stepped setbacks and corner windows,
its style is undistinguished. What makes the building unique is its
concept of adult education in combining living quarters and cultural
activities under one roof.

Its educational program offers sixteen courses of ten to twelve
weeks' duration in art, mathematics, photography, music, psychology,
and drama. The principles and techniques taught in the drama courses
are applied in productions on the stage of the 286-seat Master Theatre.
The Equity Library Theatre also uses the theatre.

Representative William Fitts Ryan pointed out in the *Congressional
Record* in 1961, on the organization's fortieth anniversary, "It should
be emphasized that the Institute is a non-profit organization and its
income from the living quarters in the building goes toward the maintenance of the museum and its adult education facilities." He also
said: "I would like to emphasize that the Master Institute is recognized
by the Board of Regents of New York State and has been given an
absolute charter. It is one of the very few private institutions to have
such a charter."

196 | The institute sponsors lectures, films, concerts, recitals, and a com-
prehensive program of museum group exhibitions. During the twenty-
year period from 1937 to 1957, the museum presented almost 160

Queen Mayadevi giving birth to Buddha; from Nepal.

shows: photography of Lewis W. Hine, Ohio artists, Mexican children's paintings, fifty prints from Uruguay, war posters, artists in service, Canadian women artists, the Negro in the arts, Danish posters, Puerto Rican artists, photographs of Bali.

The galleries for these changing exhibits are on the right of the second floor. There are three rooms spacious enough for three separate, complete exhibits. In the section at the left of the museum are two galleries for the collecton of Tibetan art. This collection has the largest group of Tankas (banner paintings) of any museum in New York. Subjects range from Buddhas in paradise, Taras, and Bodhisattvas to demons and teachers. There are also some sculptured deities, notably that of Mayadevi giving birth to Buddha.

At one time this Tibetan collection contained the *Kanjur* in 102 volumes and the *Tanjur* in 244 volumes. Both of these monumental works of Tibetan literature were presented to the Columbia University Library. The donation was made by Mr. and Mrs. Louis L. Horch, who started the Riverside Museum in 1937.

Its parent, the Master Institute of United Arts, was founded on November 17, 1921, by Nicholas Roerich for the purpose of uniting all the arts under one roof. One unit of the Master Institute was the Roerich Museum, which used to be in this building.

As Nicholas Roerich conceived it, the building was to house persons interested in culture and art who followed his doctrines. During the twenties and thirties Roerich's fantastic influence had spread throughout the world. He was revered not only as an artist but also as a mystic. The Roerich Museum and Press, the School of the Master Institute, its living quarters, the International Art Center and all the other facets of the Institute were intended to be a self-contained utopia of the arts. Roerich's aim was a "synthesis of the arts, the awakening, the nurture and development of the creative spirit," which, at any time, is a noble and worthwhile endeavor.

NICHOLAS ROERICH MUSEUM
Address: 319 West 107th St. (at Riverside Drive), New York, N.Y.
Phone: UN 4-7752

Days: Open every day, except Saturdays, 2–5.
Admission: Free.

Subway: IRT Broadway-242nd St. train to 110th St. station, south 3 blocks.

Bus: 5th Ave. (Riverside Drive) bus to 107th St.
Auto: West Side Highway to 96th St. exit, then north on Riverside Drive. Ample street parking.

Gift Shop: Postcards, publications for sale.

Special Events: Lectures on art, music, and science; concert recitals.

Membership: Membership privileges include free attendance at con-certs, bulletins, announcements.

For the past fifteen years the Nicholas Roerich Museum has occupied a former town house off Riverside Drive. Three floors of the building are devoted to the work of this artist who became known as the "Master of the Mountain" because of his paintings of Himalayan, Tibetan, and Indian mountain scenes. Anyone seeing his pictures for the first time will be startled by the strange ice-blue, chartreuse, purple, and violet colors. Roerich is represented in the Louvre and the Luxembourg Museum (Paris), the Victoria and Albert Museum (London), National Museum (Stockholm), and the Tretyakov Gallery (Moscow). His landscapes recall the work of Vasily Kandinsky or Franz Marc.

The principal objective of the museum, an incorporated nonprofit educational institution, is to "disseminate the ideals of art and culture to which the artist dedicated his life." In addition to maintaining Roerich's paintings and publicizing his ideals of peace through culture, the museum exhibits the works of some young artists, offers lectures on art, and presents recitals by concert artists.

Nicholas Konstantin Roerich was born in St. Petersburg in 1874, and studied art, philosophy, history, law, and archaeology. He painted over seven thousand pictures, of which about a hundred are on view here. He was also a mural painter and scenic designer who contributed designs for stage productions, particularly opera, in Russia. Until 1916 he directed the School for Encouraging Fine Arts in Russia. He was also connected with the Moscow Art Theater and the Diaghilev Ballet. In his lifetime he published nearly thirty volumes, besides many essays and articles. As an explorer and scientist he carried out extensive | 199 archaeological research and excavations in Russia and the Orient.

Roerich lived in Russia, Finland, and England until 1920, when the Chicago Art Institute invited him to visit America on an exhibition tour. He stayed here until 1923, when he organized and conducted a

In the Roerich Museum.

five-year expedition to India, Tibet, Mongolia, and remote areas of Central Asia. The expedition was sponsored by Roerich's Master Institute of United Arts. Roerich eventually made his home in the valley of the Punjab and lived there for eighteen years until his death in 1947.

The original collection of the museum consisted of works brought to America for his exhibition tour and others created while the artist was in America, at Monhegan, Maine; Santa Fe, New Mexico; and the Grand Canyon. In the current collection are works produced while he was in Tibet and India.

Roerich was honored in many countries. In 1929 he was nominated for a Nobel Peace Prize, based on his international campaign for better understanding and greater harmony among nations under a pact for international protection, in war or peace, of monuments, institutions, and cultural treasures. The pact was known as the Roerich Pact; its symbol, the banner of peace, utilized three red spheres within a circle. The pact was also intended to draw the attention of mankind to those values that are the common heritage of the civilized world. As of 1954, almost fifty-four nations had ratified the pact.

INTERCHURCH CENTER

Address: 475 Riverside Drive (at 119th St.), New York, N.Y.
Phone: 870-2200

Days: Open Mondays through Fridays, 9–5. Open Saturdays, Sundays, and holidays, 12 noon to 5. Closed Good Friday, Thanksgiving, Christmas, and New Year's Day.
Admission: Free.

Subway: IRT Broadway-242nd St. train to 116th St. station. Walk one block west to Riverside Drive, north to center.
Bus: 5th Ave. (Riverside Drive) bus to 119th St.
Auto: West Side Highway to 125th St. then south on Riverside Drive. Ample street parking.

Restaurant: Cafeteria in basement open to public.

Special Events: Summer film program; inquire at desk.

Tours: Groups should make reservations in advance for tours. Phone or write to Tour Information, Room 253.

A modern structure faced with Alabama limestone, the Interchurch Center looks toward Riverside Drive and the Hudson River. A piece of rock in the cornerstone is from the agora in Corinth, where "many . . . hearing Paul believed."

The entire city block on which the building stands was donated by John D. Rockefeller, Jr. The center "is a visible symbol of the oneness of many churches in Christ." Its nineteen stories house church-related organizations of the Protestant and Orthodox communions in America. Of particular interest to tourists are the Narthex, the Chapel, the Orthodox Room, and the Treasure Room, all on the street floor.

The Treasure Room, to the right of the entrance, is paneled in English oak. It has floor-to-ceiling sliding aluminum posts for display panels. From September to May art exhibitions with a religious theme are shown in the gallery.

The Narthex (a vestibule or waiting room) to the left separates the
Chapel and Orthodox Room. A strange textured tapestry hangs on the wall, and a thousand tiny lucite tubes in the ceiling light the room. The "canopy of stars" is the work of New York sculptor Israel Levitan.

The Chapel demonstrates the fine possibilities of modern design in

an ecclesiastical setting. The simplicity of the interior, the selection of white rose bricks, the arrangement of the Chi Rho (ancient Greek symbol for the Christ), and the window of translucent English alabaster create a unified, reverent effect.

The Orthodox Room displays "Byzantine Art in the Service of Christianity" with an impressive array of icons and Eastern Orthodox art objects from the collection of Paul M. Fekula, an active member of the Russian Orthodox Greek Catholic Church of America. His collection, in fifteen glass cases, is said to be one of the finest outside Russia. It features sixteenth-century icons of major holy days of the Church, a bishop's miter, vestments and altar cloths, and ancient books of Orthodox services.

MUSEUM OF THE AMERICAN INDIAN

Address: Audubon Terrace, Broadway at 155th St., New York, N.Y.
Phone: AU 3-2420

Days: Open Tuesdays through Sundays, 1–5. Closed Mondays and holidays.
Admission: Free.

Subway: (1) IRT Broadway-242nd St. train to 157th St. station. (2) IND 8th Ave. Washington Heights train to 155th St. station. Walk two blocks west to Broadway.
Auto: West Side Highway to 158th St. exit. East to Broadway, south to Audubon Terrace. Ample street parking.

Gift Shop: Books on Indians, Indian handicrafts, toys, souvenirs.

Research: Special research facilities in Bronx for scholars.

Tours: School groups welcome, but one adult must be responsible for each 10 children. No guide service.

The Museum of the American Indian is the largest Indian museum in the world. George C. Heye founded the institution, which was opened to the public in 1922. His collections form the nucleus of the museum, | 203 whose main purpose is the furthering of a better understanding of the Indians by the collection and preservation of cultural material. Support comes from a modest endowment. The institution receives no city, state, or Federal tax monies. For the public the museum offers

The Interchurch Center.

identification of specimens, technical advice, and general information. Its publications include bibliographies, ethnological studies, and definitive archaeological reports. There is a research branch of the museum in the Bronx, where the bulk of the study specimens are maintained for scholarly research purposes.

The public exhibitions at Audubon Terrace are arranged by regions —peoples of the Southeast, the Basin-Plateau region, Indians of the Plains, the Great Lakes Tribes, New England Indians. Exhibits from the tribes of each region outline the environment, the tribe's economy, housing, weapons, hunting techniques, foods, religion, social organization, games and entertainments. Exhibits interpret the life of the tribes by displaying commonplace objects side by side with rare or unique items.

Familiar tribal names are present—Iroquois, Navajo, Algonquin,

Shrunken human figures from the head-hunting Jivaro Indians of Ecuador.

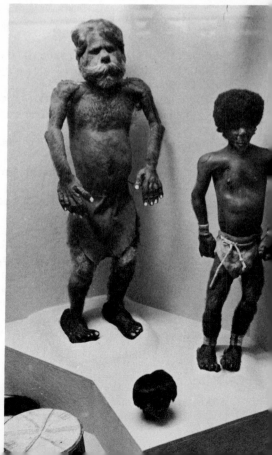

Indian baskets and beadwork.

Hopi. Seminoles are represented with the Creek, Cherokee, and other tribes in a case displaying particularly beautiful Indian dresses, plain pottery, and intricate basketweaving. The Iroquois exhibits are the most extensive to be seen anywhere. One display shows the frightening masks of the Society of False Faces. Masks represent the mythological forest creatures the Indians believed had the power to cure disease. By impersonating the powerful spirit, the man who wore the false face gained the power to cure.

Also on the first floor are some historic wampum belts. "Wampum" meant white string of shell beads. The Dutch gave Long Island the name Sewan Hacky, or "wampum land," because of the quantities of shells found there. These purple and white cylindrical shell beads

| 205

were used in trading between the Indians and the Dutch, and were made from the lip of the hardshell clam. Near the wampum case hangs an unusual parchment peace treaty made in 1765 between the British and the Delaware, Shawnee, and Mingo tribes. Small, crude animal drawings represent the mark of the tribes.

Ethnic material from the Southeast is rare, and the museum display of such specimens is unsurpassed. A section shows peyote paraphernalia and the role played by fetishes and charms. Special exhibitions are held in the gallery to the left of the museum entrance. The gift shop to the right carries a variety of authentic items, Indian basketry, books, Kachina dolls, masks, and small sculpture.

The stairway to the upper floors is hung with a number of decorated elk skins and buffalo robes. The second floor presents the ethnology of the Indians of the Southwest, a major Northwest Coast gallery depicting the California tribes, the Indians of Canada, and the Eskimos. Parts of these galleries are being reinstalled, and a major program is under way to edit these very crowded sections on ethnology and archaeology. Dominating the gallery are huge feast dishes and a whale-hunting canoe carved from a single cedar log. Whale-hunting Indians of the coast of Washington and from Vancouver Island set out in such canoes without sail or compass.

The third floor contains the Williams Hall of Middle American Archaeology. An exhibit of Panamanian Ceramic Art (1500–1000 B.C.) has some superb specimens of blue pottery, and is proof of a highly sophisticated culture in that area. Examples of sculpture, mosaic, and metalwork, especially in gold and silver, are outstanding. Newly assembled exhibits illustrate the arts of northern Mexico, Mayan life, Central American tribes, West Indies, Argentina, Brazil, Chile, Peru. The exhibits emphasize pottery, small sculpture, jewelry, clothing, weapons, musical instruments, masks, and two human bodies shrunken by the Jivaro Indians of Ecuador.

AMERICAN GEOGRAPHICAL SOCIETY

Address: Audubon Terrace, Broadway at 155th St., New York, N.Y.
Phone: AD 4-8100

206 | *Days*: Open Mondays to Fridays, 9–4:45. Closed Saturdays, Sundays.
Admission: Free.

American Geographical Society.

Subway: (1) IRT Broadway-242nd St. train to 157th St. station. (2) IND 8th Ave. Washington Heights train to 155th St. station. Walk two blocks west to Broadway.

Auto: West Side Highway to 158th St. exit. East to Broadway, south to Audubon Terrace. Ample street parking.

Membership: Seven types of membership, ranging from $10.00 annual dues upward. Membership privileges include subscription to publication and bonus maps.

The American Geographical Society is an organization with a noble history, and its possession of 160,000 bound volumes, hundreds of periodicals, 275,000 maps, 4,000 atlases, and 40,000 photographs gives it an eminent standing. Yet few people realize the existence of this vast storehouse of geographical knowledge.

Unlike the National Geographic Society in Washington, D.C. (1888), with over 4 million members, the American Geographical Society (1852) has only 4,000 members, and does not issue a popular monthly magazine with color photographs. It, however, is the oldest geographical society in the United States.

The American Geographical Society exists for the sole purpose of advancing "geography as a science, as an educational discipline, and as a guide to knowledge." In achieving its objective, the society carries out original investigations in economic and human geography, glaciology, oceanography, and cartography; it issues scientfic publications, maintains the largest private geographical library and map collection in the Western Hemisphere, presents lectures, and gives awards for exploration and geographic research. As a tax-free institution, it is open to the public, principally to college students and researchers "who know exactly what they are looking for."

The society is housed in the same Classic Eclectic style as the other museums in Audubon Terrace. The street floor has one exhibition gallery and the World Data Center of Glaciology. The library and card catalogue are on the second floor. The map room on the third floor has maps and charts from all over the world, dating from ancient times to the present. The maps cover everything from topographical structure, political communities, plant-life dispersement, glacial makeup —just about any kind of map imaginable. On the fourth floor the cartographers' skylight studio is busy with classified work for the space program.

THE HISPANIC SOCIETY OF AMERICA

Address: Audubon Terrace, Broadway at 155th St., New York, N.Y.
Phone: WA 6-2234

Days: Tuesdays through Saturdays, 10–4:30; Sundays, 2–5. Library
open Tuesdays through Fridays, 1–4:30; Saturdays, 10–4:30. Closed
Mondays, July 4th, Thanksgiving, Christmas, and New Year's Day.
Admission: Free.

Subway: (1) IRT Broadway-242nd St. train to 157th St. station. (2)
IND 8th Ave. Washington Heights train to 155th St. station; walk
two blocks west to Broadway.
Auto: West Side Highway to 158th St. exit. East to Broadway, south
to Audubon Terrace. Ample street parking.

Gift Shop: Museum shop sells publications of society, color prints and
slides and postcards.

Tours: Acoustiguide recorded tour enables visitors to hear lecture on
Spanish art while walking in the museum. Fee $.50 for one person,
$.75 for two.

As darkly magnificent, cool, and hushed as the interior of a Spanish
grandee's castle, the Hispanic Museum sits in splendor, the ruby-red
jewel of Audubon Terrace. In front of the museum the terrace courtyard is dominated by a statue of Spain's national hero, El Cid. The
eleventh-century warrior has been re-created as he might have appeared at the siege of Valencia. This piece, and the animal and figure
bronzes, stone lions at the museum door, and limestone reliefs of Don
Quixote and Boabdil on the courtyard wall were all created by Anna
Hyatt Huntington, wife of the museum's founder. She is still active
today, and recently unveiled a huge bronze of a Cuban statesman at
the foot of Central Park.

Archer Milton Huntington made his first trip to the Iberian Penin-
sula in 1892. From an archaeological camp at Italica, the first Roman
colony in Spain, near Seville, he brought home Corinthian capitals,
inscribed gravestone fragments, and jewelry. His collection includes | 209
sculpture and pottery from Roman times; tiles, metalwork, and textiles
from the period of Moorish domination; and Gothic and Renaissance
art from the Christian era.

Since childhood Huntington's thoughts had dwelt on "the founda-

Main hall of the Hispanic museum.

tion of a Hispanic center where source material in documents and examples of the arts of Spain and Portugal might be studied as a basis for original research." In 1904, he established the Hispanic Society. Two years later he donated land near Audubon Terrace for a Spanish church, a site that was known at the turn of the century as Spanish Hill. The Church, Our Lady of Esperanza, has become an important institution where Puerto Rican immigrants can find help in learning English, finding work, and adapting to their new environment while preserving the traditional faith.

The Indiana limestone façade of the museum building is enhanced by sculptural and architectural detail. The museum's collections consist of prehistoric art through the Visigothic period, Hispano-Moresque,

The Hispanic Society of America.

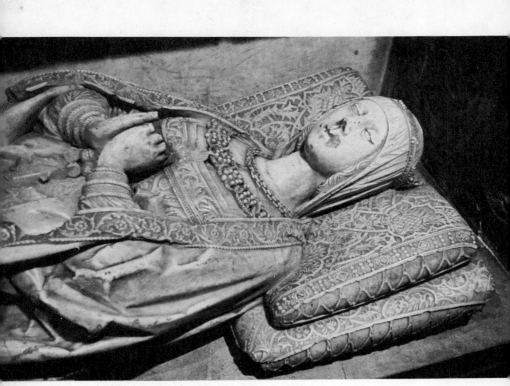

16th-century tomb of the Duchess of Alburquerque.

Mudejar, Gothic, Renaissance, baroque, rococo, and neoclassic art, and nineteenth- and twentieth-century paintings.

The library of the Hispanic Society contains about 12,000 books printed before 1701. It also has a collection of maps, globes, incunabula, Bibles, liturgies, chronicles, books on chivalry, codes of law, and some 90,000 other books relating to the art, history, and society of Spain, Portugal, and colonial Hispanic America. In the anteroom of the library are hand-carved mahogany choir stalls.

The main gallery on the street floor is two stories high. The entire room is decorated in the flat red terra-cotta typical of the Spanish Renaissance. Daylight filters into the gallery from an ornamental skylight in the beamed ceiling. Twenty archways surrounding the room

Spanish tiles and pottery.

separate it from an encircling corridor. Roman sculpture is placed in some of the archways, whose pillars rest on red marble. Each sustaining arch has an escutcheon bearing the arms of a province or city of Spain. Within the arcades are panels from fourteenth- and fifteenth-century Catalan, Valencian, and Leonese retablos, polychrome wood carvings, ivories, samples of gold a'nd silverwork, laces and textiles. One section of the corridor is devoted to the magnificent alabaster and marble tomb of the Duchess of Alburquerque. Inside the gallery hang paintings by Goya and Velázquez.

Off the main gallery a small room of mosaics leads to the gallery where modern landscapes surround the entire room. The artist, Joaquin Sorolla y Bastida (1863–1923), was honored with a major exhibit here in 1909. His 350 paintings attracted nearly 160,000 visitors in one month. These paintings, commissioned in 1911, depict occupations, activities, and ceremonies of the various Spanish provinces.

The upstairs stairway glitters with Hispano-Moresque ceramic tiles and stone fragments. In the west wing are modern paintings mounted under glass. In the east wing are displays of rugs, gold, velvet brocades. There are Goya prints and watercolors, including examples of his "Caprices." These galleries also display a superb collection of colored engravings of the ritual of the bullfight as seen by artists from the fifteenth century to Picasso's aquatints of 1958. An outstanding bullfight sequence was etched by Goya. There are posters, photographs, books, and programs of bullfighting, architectural studies of bullrings, announcements, displays of weapons, banderillas, and so on.

The balcony that overlooks the main gallery is lined with a gorgeous miscellany of bronze door knockers, Roman glassware, vases, lusterware, huge Gothic tiles, and paintings by Velázquez, El Greco, and Ribera.

THE AMERICAN NUMISMATIC SOCIETY
Address: Audubon Terrace, Broadway at 155th St., New York, N.Y.
Phone: AU 6-3030

Days: Open Tuesdays through Saturdays, 9–5. Closed Sundays, Mondays, and holidays.

214 | *Admission:* Free.

Subway: (1) IRT Broadway-242nd St. train to 157th St. station. (2) IND 8th Ave. Washington Heights train to 155th St. station. Walk two blocks west to Broadway.

Auto: West Side Highway to 158th St. exit. East to Broadway, south
to Audubon Terrace. Ample street parking.

Library: Open 9–5.

Inside the heavy bronze doors of the American Numismatic Society,
to the left, are exhibits of the world's coinage. To the right are medals
and decorations. On the second floor is the most comprehensive numismatic library in America, with particular emphasis on periodicals and
international auction catalogues.

The society was organized on April 16, 1858, and is "devoted to
the advancement of numismatic knowledge, especially as it relates to
history, art, archaeology and economics," by engaging in the collection of coins, medals, tokens, decorations, and paper money. The

American Numismatic Society (rear left).

society offers a vast number of numismatic publications of the highest scholarly quality. It holds summer seminars in numismatics to provide students with an understanding of how this science applies to other fields of knowledge. Some grants-in-aid, as well as achievement awards, are given. At various times the society has struck its own commemorative medals. Governed and managed by a council of fifteen members, the society has four classes of membership.

The only museum in the world devoted entirely to numismatics, its major exhibition space illustrates the development of coinage since the first coins were introduced some 2,600 years ago. The history of coins is shown in sixteen specially designed display cases that contain enlarged photographs, maps, and explanatory texts.

The museum's wealth of coins from the ancient Greek, Roman, and Byzantine periods derives from the extraordinary collection of over 87,000 pieces bequeathed by Edward T. Newell, president of the society from 1916 to his death in 1941. Other private gifts have further enriched the collections, while a relatively small proportion of the coins were acquired by purchase. Also represented are Italian Renaissance and medieval German coins.

The latest period in coinage history is represented by a numismatic genealogy of England, America, and the new nations of Israel, Libya, Indonesia, Burma, and Pakistan. In the East Gallery a case contains an extremely rare series of large United States copper cents struck from 1793–1857, a gift of George A. Clapp; some Lincoln medals and slave identification tags.

The West Gallery displays medals and medallions. There are Indian peace medals, exposition medals, United States decorations, British Orders of Knighthood, and medals commemorating individuals of note. The plate-sized Waterloo Medallion was designed by the distinguished Italian coin engraver Benedetto Pistrucci. Chief Engineer at the London mint, he was commissioned in 1817 to execute a medallion commemorating Napoleon's defeat at Waterloo. It took him thirty years to complete the dies for his elaborate plan.

THE AMERICAN ACADEMY OF ARTS AND LETTERS

216 | *Address:* Audubon Terrace, Broadway at 155th St., New York, N.Y. *Phone:* AU 6-1480

Days: Open daily, 1–5. Closed Mondays and some holidays.
Admission: Free.

The American Academy of Arts and Letters.

Subway (1) IRT Broadway-242nd St. train to 157th St. station and Broadway. (2) IND 8th Ave. Washington Heights train to 155th St. station. Walk two blocks west to Broadway.

Auto: West Side Highway to 158th St. exit. East to Broadway, south to Audubon Terrace. Ample street parking.

The American Academy of Arts and Letters and its parent body, the National Institute of Arts and Letters, are the two highest honor societies of the creative arts in this country. The National Institute, founded in 1898, consists of 250 Americans who are writers, poets, | 217 painters, sculptors, composers, or architects. The American Academy, established in 1904, is made up of 50 institute members chosen for special distinction. Both organizations are chartered by an Act of Congress.

Original manuscripts of Glenway Wescott.

Among well-known Academy members are Pearl S. Buck, Thomas Hart Benton, Aaron Copland, John Dos Passos, Lillian Hellman, Edward Hopper, Jacques Lipchitz, Walter Lippmann, Georgia O'Keeffe, Carl Sandburg, John Steinbeck, Norman Mailer, and Andrew Wyeth.

Each year the institute and academy honor distinguished accomplishment in the fields of art. Older artists may be cited for their life's work, while a very few young men and women are given awards and grants to assist them in the pursuit of their careers. New members and award winners are also honored by an exhibition of their work.

An annual art exhibition of paintings, graphics, sculpture, and architecture is shown in the art gallery on the north side of Audubon Terrace; the annual literary exhibition is held in the enormous gallery on the south side of Audubon Terrace. There are original manuscripts, notebooks, first editions, and musical scores that may be followed by means of earphones. The vast library collection of first editions and original manuscripts of academy members is available for reference on request and by appointment.

MORRIS–JUMEL MANSION
Address: West 160th St. and Edgecombe Ave., New York, N.Y.
Phone: WA 3-8008

Days: Open daily, except Monday, 11–5.
Admission: Free.

Subway: (1) IND 8th Ave. Washington Heights train to 163rd St.

station. Use 161st St. exit. Walk one block east. (2) IRT Broadway-242nd St. train to 157th St. station. Walk north to 160th St., east one block.

Auto: (1) FDR (East River) Drive to 125th St.; west on 125th St. to St. Nicholas Ave., north to 160th St., east one block. (2) West Side Highway to 158th St. exit. North to 160th St., then east. Ample street parking.

Restaurant: Picnic parties welcome in rear garden.

The Morris–Jumel Mansion is on Washington Heights, bordering Sugar Hill. This quietly residential, tree-lined section of north Harlem owes its name to its elevation, the highest in Manhattan, and to the fact that it was once an exclusive part of town. From the grounds you can see the Bronx, Queens, and lower Manhattan.

The majestic house, perched atop a layer of glacial rock, is named after its two notable tenants, Lieutenant-Colonel Roger Morris and Stephen Jumel. Morris, an aide-de-camp to the British General Edward Braddock during the French and Indian War, was a friend of George Washington. When he returned from that war, Morris married the wealthy Mary Philipse, whose name had been linked romantically with Washington. Morris built the Georgian-Colonial mansion in 1765 as a summer home. In 1775 Morris, a Tory, fled to England.

During the Revolution the house quartered both American and British forces. George Washington made Jumel Mansion his headquarters in 1776, when the Revolutionary Army was retreating after the disastrous defeat on Long Island. It had become a tavern by the time Washington paid a nostalgic visit to the house after the war.

Stephen Jumel, a wealthy French wine merchant living on Whitehall Street, bought the property in 1810 for $10,000. He and his socially ambitious wife restored the house in the most magnificent style of the nineteenth century. They entertained so lavishly that "lordly as a Jumel banquet" became a popular phrase of the day. In 1832 Jumel died, and his widow became one of the richest women in America.

Some time before her husband's death Madame Jumel had met Aaron Burr. After Jumel died, Burr apparently decided to restore his solvency by marrying the wealthy widow. His suit was successful and on July 1, 1833, they were wed. Burr was then seventy-seven years old. In Madame Jumel, Burr found more than a match for his own temper and will. A brief and stormy married life was followed by a

Morris–Jumel Mansion.

separation that lasted until Burr's death three years after the marriage. Madame Jumel lived to be ninety-three. She died in 1865 and was buried in Trinity Church cemetery at Broadway and 155th Street.

Today the entrance to the grounds, from cobblestoned Jumel Terrace, leads to the side of the building. The mansion faces south. Four impressive columns, two stories high, frame the entrance. An unusual balcony projects over the front door. The interior tastefully combines the best of Georgian, Federal, and French Empire styles. All the window draperies were woven according to period patterns and donated by Franco Scalamandre.

The small parlor to the left of the front door was the scene of Madame Jumel's marriage to Burr. In the Georgian dining room on the right the table is set. Of particular interest are the wall moldings, semi-elliptical archways, and the wide staircase to the upper floors.

On the second story a children's nursery, originally a dressing room, adjoins Madame Jumel's bedroom. The original bed and two chairs, covered in gold damask, were owned by Napoleon. A mannequin standing in the center of the room wears a copy of one of Madame Jumel's silk dresses. Aaron Burr's room, across the hall, contains his trunk and his desk-table.

In the living room.

To the rear of the house is the office of the curator, Mrs. LeRoy Campbell, whose knowledge of antiques, art, and history has proven so valuable in acquiring authentic furnishings for this splendid house. She will lead small groups touring the house, explain its history, and point out its secret passageways.

The rear rooms over the drawing room were Washington's private quarters where he slept, planned maneuvers, and wrote his reports to Congress. Handwoven blankets confiscated from a British tent lie on a replica of his camp bed.

The third floor serves as a repository for a collection of Staffordshire ware, spinning wheels, and equipment for making wax candles.

The city acquired the property and opened the museum in 1907, under the custodianship of the Washington Headquarters Association of the Daughters of the American Revolution. A bench-lined walk circles the property, and leads past a small garden in the back of the house.

THE CLOISTERS

Address: Fort Tryon Park, New York, N.Y.
Phone: WA 3-3700

Days: Open Tuesday through Saturday, 10–5; Sundays, 1–5. (May to September, Sundays, 1–6.) Closed Mondays.
Admission: Free.

Subway: IND 8th Ave. Washington Heights train to 190th St.-Overlook Terrace (elevator exit). Connects with bus to Cloisters.
Auto: Henry Hudson Pkwy. to first exit past George Washington Bridge, marked "The Cloisters, Fort Tryon." Free parking on premises, limited to three hours.

Gift Shop: Information Desk sells museum publications, etc.

Special Events: Concerts of recorded medieval music Sundays and Tuesdays at 3:30.

222 | *Membership:* Membership privileges include Garden Party, special concerts.

Tours: Tours every Wednesday at 3. Free guidance for classes from New York City public or private schools. School groups in chartered buses must have permit to enter park.

The Cloisters.

*The ciborium
in the Langon Chapel.*

Going to the Cloisters on the peak of Fort Tryon Park is the next best thing to being in a medieval monastery in France. Its medieval herb garden, rampart walks, Belgian cobblestoned courts, view of the Hudson and of the New Jersey Palisades beyond, vividly re-create, in the twentieth century, the spirit of medieval Europe.

The Cloisters, a branch of the Metropolitan Museum of Art, includes parts of the cloisters of five French monasteries, a Romanesque chapel, an original chapter house, Gothic chapels, and exhibition galleries, all chronologically arranged and constructed to incorporate the original structural elements. Within the setting are examples of sculpture, painting, stained glass, retables, tapestries, metalwork, and furniture that are ideally seen on a weekday morning. When the galleries are empty, the supreme simplicity and lack of clutter emphasize the architectural forms and the serene atmosphere. Both the buildings and works of art represent various artistic styles of two periods of the Middle Ages—the Romanesque, as exemplified by

In the Gothic Chapel.

works from monasteries, and the Gothic, as exemplified by relics
from churches.

The Cloisters collection was started by George Grey Barnard, a
sculptor. He spent many years in France seeking examples of medieval
art in barns, farmhouses, and cellars near abandoned churches and
monasteries. In 1914 he put the collection on display in a building
on nearby Fort Washington Avenue. The Metropolitan Museum
bought the collection in 1925 with funds provided by John D. Rockefeller, Jr. When Fort Tryon Park, an area of sixty-two acres, was
given to the city by Rockefeller in 1930, part was set aside for the
museum. The gift was in accordance with an agreement between the
philanthropist and the city, whereby the eastern ends of 64th and
68th Streets were closed and conveyed to the Rockefeller Institute for
Medical Research. Land along the Palisades across the Hudson was
also acquired by Rockefeller to ensure the view from the ramparts
of the Cloisters.

*Listening to music
in the Cuxa Cloister.*

Visitors interested in proceeding through the Cloisters in chronological order should start with the Romanesque Hall and continue to the Fuentiduena Chapel, St. Guilhem Cloister, Langon Chapel, the West Terrace, Chapter House, Cuxa Cloister, Nine Heroes Tapestry Room, Early Gothic Hall, and thence to the ground floor. From here proceed to the Gothic Chapel, Bonnefont Cloister, Trie Cloister, Glass Gallery, and then the Treasury. The stairway here leads to the Boppart Room, the Unicorn Tapestries, the Burgos Tapestries, the Spanish Room, Late Gothic Hall, and then out through the Froville Arcade, or main entrance hall.

A cloister is an unroofed space enclosed by a vaulted passageway consisting of colonnades or arcades opening on the court. Cloisters served both as sheltered access to other buildings and as a recreational and social area for monasteries.

The central and largest cloister here is that of St. Michel de Cuxa. It is an enclosed rectangular garden, open to the sky and surrounded

Arcades and garden court of the Trie Cloister.

A silver-gilt and enamel shrine made in Paris about 1340,
now on display in the Treasury of the Cloisters.

by pink marble arches and columns that date before 1188. Concerts of medieval recorded music are held here on Sundays. During the fall three apple trees in the center of the cloister bear dozens of delicious apples. An unusually grotesque face set in the marble wall fountain of the arcade came from the monastery of Notre-Dame du Vilar. The other cloisters are those of St. Guilhem-le-Désert (1206), identified by the potted plants in the center of the court and a modern overhead glass skylight. The Bonnefont en Comminges, founded in 1136, and the Trie Cloisters are popular both because of the herb garden and their position overlooking the Hudson River.

The Gothic Chapel contains a notable alabaster sculpture from the tomb effigy of Jean d'Alluye, who died about 1248. A life-size figure

"The Unicorn in Captivity," seventh in the
great series of Unicorn Tapestries.

represents the young man, fully armed, lying with hands joined on his breast in an attitude of prayer. His feet rest against a marble lion, symbol of courage. In the center of the chapel are three stained-glass windows, of which the middle panel is original. In the two new panels modern glassmaking techniques have not been able to duplicate the original off-white tone of the metallic ores used in the Middle Ages. Twelfth-century windows were characterized by rich, dark colors, single figures, and scrollwork; by the beginning of the thirteenth century, figures were used singly and also in groups.

The Early Gothic Hall contains a number of painted and gilded stone and wood sculptures of bishops, kings, and Virgins in thirteenth-century Gothic style. The Virgin and Child at the end of the gallery, one of the finest statues from the Île-de-France, is in an extraordinarily fine state of preservation.

The most notable feature of the Romanesque Hall is the entrance doorway from the Abbey of Moutiers Saint Jean, with life-size figures of King Clovis and his son King Clotaire on each side. Throughout the history of ecclesiastical architecture the entrance door to the cathedral has possessed a special importance. In medieval texts the church door is referred to as the Gate of Heaven, the Portal of Glory, the Triumphal Gate. The three portals incorporated in the Romanesque Hall exemplify the long evolution of these sculptured portals.

The Hall of the Unicorn Tapestries contains a set of six hand-woven fifteenth-century textiles that are among the most prized of our inheritances from the Middle Ages. The tapestries were given to the museum by John D. Rockefeller, Jr., in 1935. Depicting the Hunt of the Unicorn, they are thought to portray an allegory of the life of Christ, who is supposed to be represented by the fabulous Unicorn, symbol of purity. Other authorities hold that the Hunt is an allegory of secular courtship and love. The tapestries are remarkable for their beautiful color and design and the intensity and vitality of their pictorial realism. It is believed that all but one were woven for Anne of Brittany, in celebration of her marriage to Louis XII on January 8, 1499.

The Treasury contains some of the earliest and most precious objects that have survived from the Middle Ages: the Chalice of Antioch, reliquary statuettes, Limoges enamels, bronzes, the Monkey Cup, Book of Hours of Jeanne d'Évreux, and the recently acquired silver-gilt and enamel shrine made by Parisian goldsmiths about 1340 and believed to have been the personal possession of Queen Elizabeth of Hungary.

A view of the Bonnefont Cloister.

DYCKMAN HOUSE

Address: Broadway and 204th St., New York, N.Y.
Phone: (Department of Parks) RE 4-1000

Days: Daily 10–5. Closed Mondays. Children under 16 not admitted
unless accompanied by an adult.
Admission: Free.

Subway: (1) IND 8th Ave. Washington Heights train to 207th St.
Leave train by south exit, walk one block south. (2) IRT Broad-
way-242nd St. train to 207th St. station; walk west up the hill to
Broadway, then one block south.
Auto: Henry Hudson Pkwy. to Dyckman St. exit. East to Broadway,
then north to 204th St. Ample street parking; meters on Broadway.

Dyckman House.

Dyckman House, set on a slight hill, is surrounded by supermarkets, apartment houses, and gas stations. It is a civic miracle that the original eighteenth-century farmhouse has survived the inroads of twentieth-century progress to become today the only Dutch Colonial farmhouse remaining in Manhattan.

William Dyckman inherited the estate from his grandfather, who built the first house here in 1748. During the Revolution it was burned by the British and rebuilt in its present form in 1783. In 1915, two descendants of Dyckman purchased the property, restored the house and grounds, and presented them to the city.

All the Dutch and English Colonial furnishings, clothes, china, and ornaments are authentic period pieces. The interior is relatively modest, and represents the ordinary style of living in New York at that time. The kitchen, with its caldrons, pothooks, irons, skillets, and ovens is the most interesting of the five rooms.

A large Indian village once flourished in the vicinity of present-day Inwood Park, a short distance away, and Indians remained in the vicinity well into the nineteenth century. In fact, a walk four blocks north and then four blocks east brings you to Indian Road and West 215th Street. Continuing across the open field of Inwood Park to a spot near the cliffs, you will find a large boulder marking the site of the principal Manhattan Indian village of Shorakkopoch. Here Peter Minuit purchased Manhattan Island from the Indians in 1626 for trinkets and beads worth then about 60 guilders ($24.00).

VAN CORTLANDT HOUSE MUSEUM

Address: Van Cortlandt Park, Broadway near 242nd St., New York, N.Y.

Phone: KI 6-3323

Days: Open Tuesdays through Saturdays, 10–5; Sundays, 2–5. Closed Mondays and month of February.

Admission: $.25 on Sunday, Tuesday, Wednesday, and Thursday. Other days free.

Subway: IRT Broadway-242nd St. train to 242nd St. station (last stop).

Auto: (1) From FDR (East River) Drive north to Willis Ave. Bridge. Major Deegan Expressway to 238th St. exit. Continue west to Broadway. Right turn onto Broadway. House visible from outside

Van Cortlandt Mansion.

park, on Broadway, near 246th St. (2) From Henry Hudson Pkwy., Route 9 exist south (Broadway) to 246th St. Ample parking.

Like other important and wealthy men of his era, Frederick Van Cortlandt built his manor in 1748 with his own labor force—carpenters, masons, and blacksmiths. The elegant Georgian-Colonial mansion was a country estate where flax was woven and spun, stock raised, and crops planted. In the 1740's the inhabited section of New York City extended to Canal Street. North of Canal were farms and forests.

The mansion was built of rough stone with brick trimming. Satyr-like carved faces are set as keystones above the windows. Carved-face keystones of this genre also appeared later in New York tenements of the period 1890 to 1910. Many can be seen on the Lower East Side, but these particular early faces are unique in Colonial architecture. Since all the faces are different, it is possible they were carved on the spot by an enterprising stonemason, rather than imported from Europe. The windows under the keystones once had shutters, but they have all been removed, as have the Dutch half-doors.

The house is surrounded by a high wrought-iron fence. Once you are inside, it is apparent that the house has an English atmosphere with Dutch accents. The exhibition room, for example, contains a fine collection of Delftware. This room was originally a dining room,

The east parlor, to the right of the entrance, has a Georgian mantel, a handsome secretary of Massachusetts origin that contains an unusual Whieldon tea set; a spinet that was made in London in 1771, and a Chippendale mirror that is dated 1760. The dining room, formerly the west parlor, was occupied by General George Washington in 1783 when the area from Vault Hill (behind the house) to Kingsbridge was the scene of almost constant skirmishing.

The kitchen, below ground level, has a huge fireplace, caldrons, kettle, long-handled peels, or oven shovels for drawing out hot bread pans, and curious waffle irons. The southeast bedroom, upstairs, is where Washington slept. The room has a typical canopied bed and a cherry writing desk. There is also a seventeenth-century Dutch bedroom with a bed completely enclosed in wood to ward off the cold air. A | 235 walnut wardrobe (Dutch *kas*), elaborately painted in grisaille, held linens. The nursery on the third floor contains an Early American dollhouse. In the spinning room next door are fifteen-inch-wide floorboards that were handmade and are held together by wooden pegs.

THE HALL OF FAME FOR GREAT AMERICANS
Address: 181st Street and University Avenue, Bronx, N.Y.
Phone: UN 1-2175

Days: Open daily, 9-5, including Sundays and holidays.
Admission: Free.

Subway: IRT Broadway or Lexington Ave. Jerome-Woodlawn train to
Burnside Ave. station.
Auto: FDR (East River) Drive via Willis Ave. Bridge to Bronx. Left
onto Major Deegan Expressway, north to Fordham Road exit.
Continue on Fordham Road to University Avenue. Right to 181st
St. Right again, up hill to stone posts marking New York Univer-

The Hall of Fame.

sity campus. Enter gate. Hall of Fame on right directly past parking lot. Free parking.

Tour: Tour disks relate history of famous men. Official handbook published by the university relates story of founding, brief biographies of famous men.

The Hall of Fame for Great Americans is on the uptown campus of New York University. Designed by Stanford White and financed as a gift to the university by Mrs. Finley J. Shepard, the Hall of Fame consists of an open-air colonnade, 630 feet long. It was dedicated in 1901. The Cloisters at Fort Tryon Park can be seen in the distance. Within the colonnade are the silent bronze heads facing each other, row after row. All eyes stare unnervingly at some point above the visitor's head . . . all the determined chins thrust forward.

To become eligible for nomination one must have been dead at least twenty-five years and also have contributed to the history, culture, or development of the United States. In a recent year there were 225 nominations submitted to the Hall of Fame Committee. Selections are made every five years. Elections are held by a College of Electors chosen by the university, and the electors represent all states of the Union and a wide variety of professions.

At present the Hall of Fame honors eighty-nine Americans, including Eli Howe, Alexander Graham Bell, Robert Fulton, Thomas A. Edison, Tom Paine, Benjamin Franklin, George Washington, Henry Clay, Abraham Lincoln, and so on.

POE COTTAGE
Address: Poe Park, Grand Concourse at East 193rd St., Bronx, N.Y.
Phone: 828-3200 (Bronx Parks Dept.)

Days: Open Tuesday-Saturday, 10–1 and 2–5; Sunday, 1–5. Closes 4:00 in winter. Closed holidays.
Admission: Free.

Subway: IND 6th Ave. "D" train to Fordham Road station. Walk one block north on Grand Concourse to Poe Park.
Auto: FDR (East River) Drive north to Willis Ave. Bridge, Major Deegan Expressway. At Fordham Road exit, turn right. Continue past Grand Concourse one block, then go left at Valentine Ave. to Poe Park. Metered street parking.

Poe Cottage.

Poe Cottage, the home of Edgar Allan Poe from 1846 to 1849, is a small country house with a single story and an attic. It was built by John Wheeler about 1812 as a farmhouse. The city acquired the cottage in 1912 and moved it from Kingsbridge Road to Poe Park.

The cottage is sparsely furnished, and only the three rooms on the lower floor are open to the public. They comprise a small hand-carved four-poster bed and dresser, a writing desk, rocker, hooked rugs, Franklin stove, cupboard, two wall clocks, a table and two kitchen chairs, and a large cabinet with Staffordshire platters and tureens.

Poe's young wife, Virginia, died in this house, where he wrote "The Literati of New York City" for *Godey's Lady's Book* and his famous poems "Annabel Lee," "Ulalume," and "Eureka." After his wife's death, in 1847, Poe fell in love successively with several women, and was once engaged to Sarah Helen Whitman, as well as to his boyhood sweetheart Elmira Shelton. Poe died on October 1, 1849.

Today the Poe Cottage has no caretaker or authoritative guide. The house sits quietly in a little-frequented corner of a city park, as much overlooked by the passerby as it must have been during his lifetime.

NEW YORK BOTANICAL GARDEN
Address: Bronx Park, Bronx, N.Y.
Phone: LU 4-8500

Days: Daily, including holidays, from 10 to a half hour after sunset.
 Museum and conservatories close at 4:30.
Admission: Free.

Subway: (1) IND 6th Ave. "D" train to Bedford Park Blvd. station. Use south exit and walk east eight blocks. (2) IRT 7th Ave. East Bronx express, or Lexington Ave. East Bronx express to 149th St. station. Get off train and transfer to 3rd Ave. elevated train; get off at 200th St. and walk east one block.
Railroad: From Grand Central Station take New York Central Harlem Division to Botanical Garden station. Main entrance opposite station.
Auto: Main roads approaching garden are marked with New York Botanical Garden signs. Follow: (1) Bronx River Pkwy. to Mosholu Pkwy. or Pelham Pkwy. (2) Hutchinson River Pkwy. to Pelham Pkwy. (3) New England Thruway to Pelham Pkwy. (4) Henry Hudson Pkwy. to Mosholu Pkwy. (5) Grand Concourse to

Bedford Park Blvd. Main entrance is on Southern Blvd., near Fordham University. Cars can enter garden free on weekdays. $1.00 entrance fee for cars Saturdays, Sundays, and holidays. Parking permitted throughout garden.

Restaurant: Snuff Mill Cafeteria has hot food, snacks, sandwiches. Outdoor terrace. Picnic tables near restaurant. Snuff Mill open from Saturday before Palm Sunday until Saturday after Thanksgiving.

Gift Shop: Sales counter near museum entrance offers publications. Another counter in the greenhouse sells plants.

Special Events: Seasonal displays throughout the year. Some of the major attractions are the Pot Plant Show (January), Easter Show, Rose Day, Chrysanthemum Show (November), and the Christmas Show.

Membership: Privileges include subscription to *The Garden Journal,* invitations to flower shows, tours, lectures, reduced rates for courses, free professional advice on gardening problems, etc.

Library: Major reference and research center for botanists, on third floor of museum, contains 70,000 volumes, 300,000 pamphlets. Open to public for reference, not lending. Research Laboratory building not open to public.

Lectures and Tours: Public-education program with two-year certificated courses in gardening, landscape gardening, and botany. Free lecture series and day and evening courses for adults.

Children: Special children's courses include a late spring-summer gardencraft course in which the children plant and tend their own plants and take home their produce in the fall.

". . . I will look upon thy face again, my own romantic Bronx. And it will be a face more pleasant than the face of men. . . ." This legend by the poet Joseph Rodman Drake appears on a bronze plaque fastened on a boulder that stands beneath a footbridge by the old Snuff Mill.

The gorge of the rapid Bronx River, complete with its ten-foot waterfall, glacial rock, hemlock forest, and towering trees has probably

The rotunda of the greenhouse, New York Botanical Garden.

The old snuff mill.

changed little since the poet wrote those words. The stream runs through the middle of the Botanical Garden.

Since the gorge is one of the most attractive features of the garden, it is natural to find along the bank a terraced restaurant overlooking the river, footpath, and waterfall. The building was once the Lorillard Snuff Mill, built here in 1840. Snuff was ground and tobacco packed in this factory building.

Another attractive feature of the garden is that it is possible to drive directly into it. Following the Circuit Drive, you can see fields of daffodils and lilacs, magnolias and roses, the Snuff Mill, the Museum, and the conservatory. There are 230 acres of garden.

Near the main entrance is the museum, housed in New York City civic architecture of the 1890's. The museum has mostly permanent exhibits. To the left of the door are Food Plants—coconut, fruit, teas, cocoa, wheat, spices, sugar. A series of excellent English colored lithographs depicts the cultivation of rice in China. The right-hand gallery shows plant families, plant evolution, tree leaves, flower families, seed

Giant plants in the greenhouse.

distribution, cycad evolution, and flower structure. All the exhibits are arranged in clear and simple order.

The second floor contains hundreds and hundreds of ceiling-high steel lockers packed with legal-size file folders containing dried plants. This extraordinary herbarium of 3 million plants seems to include every plant of North and South America, and on the third floor is a herbarium of local plants. The vast botanical and horticultural library, which ranks among the three best in the Western Hemisphere, has just been installed in a brand new six-story building called the Harriet Barnes Pratt Library Wing. The library receives twelve hundred current periodicals on botany. The librarians welcome visitors, and will permit them to examine the botanical specimens in the herbar-

The gorge of the Bronx River.

ium. Across the drive from the museum is the modern research laboratory. Visitors are not permitted to enter.

The magnificent glass-domed rotunda of the great greenhouse is visible from the main entrance. As the visitor enters the conservatories he encounters a heavy, subtropical, unmistakably jungle atmosphere. An immense sugar palm tree shoots straight up into the rotunda (ninety feet high). There are tropical trees from Africa, Brazil, Australia. In the hushed quiet of this tropical foliage one can easily hear the low drone of the IRT subway.

To the left of the palm house are winding paths leading to eleven other greenhouses, which contain, among other specimens, ground ivy, tropical flowering and foliage plants, hanging baskets, lime bushes; fig, grapefruit, apple, and plum trees; strange screw pines, bromeliads, cissus and fern plants, and, in a ninety-nine degree hothouse, ageless cactus plants in all shades of green. In the courtyard in front of the greenhouses are the water-lily ponds.

The garden, incorporated in 1891, was patterned after the Royal Botanic Gardens at Kew, England. Its purposes, according to the Act of Incorporation, are the collection and culture of plants, the advancement of botanical science, and the entertainment, recreation, and instruction of the people.

NEW YORK ZOOLOGICAL PARK (BRONX ZOO)
Address: 185th St. and Southern Blvd., Bronx, N.Y.
Phone: WE 3-1500

Days: Opens at 10 daily. Closes at 4:30 in winter, 6:30 in summer.
Admission: Free daily, *except* Tuesdays, Wednesdays, Thursdays. Children over 5 and adults, $.25. Free on all legal holidays.

Entrances: Main—Pelham Pkwy. Others—Fordham, Crotona, Boston Road, Buffalo, Bronxdale.
Subway: (1) IRT 7th Ave.: Dyre Ave. or East 180th St. Express to 177th St. (2) IRT Lexington Ave.: White Plains Road Express to 177th St. (3) IND 6th Ave.: "D" train to Fordham Road, then bus to Fordham Gate.
Auto: (1) FDR (East River) Drive to Bruckner Blvd., Hutchinson River Pkwy. Exit to Pelham Pkwy., Bronx Zoo. (2) Henry Hudson Pkwy., Exit 18 to Mosholu Pkwy., Exit 7 to Bronx River Pkwy. to Bronx Zoo.
Parking: (1) Fountain Circle: Main entrance off Pelham Pkwy.

Entrance to the Bronx Zoo.

(2) Bronxdale: Alongside Bronx River Pkwy.
(3) Crotona: At 182nd St. and Southern Blvd.
(4) Buffalo: Bronx Park South and Boston Road (closed in winter-time).
Fee: Weekdays $.50; Saturdays, Sundays, holidays, $.75.

Restaurants: (1) Cafeteria: hot and cold dishes, complete meals.
(2) Zoo Terrace Buffet: salads, sandwiches, snacks.
(3) Flamingo Terrace: sandwiches, snacks.
(4) African Terrace: sandwiches, snacks.
(5) Lake Terrace: picnic parties, snacks.
(6) Carretinas: soda, ice cream, snacks.

Gift Shop: Souvenirs, books, pennants, toys at Question House. Souvenirs also at stand near sea-lion pool.

Feeding Times:

Pelicans	11	summer only
Penguin pool	2:30	daily
Penguin house	3	daily
Alligators	3	Mondays, Wednesdays, Fridays
Sea lions	3	except Mondays
Bird walk	3:15	summer only
Lion house	3:30	except Mondays
Otter pool	3:30	winter at 2

Membership: Annual, $15.00. Special privileges to society members.

Tours: Tiger Train tours, May-August, daily except Sundays and Mondays, start near sea-lion pool. Adults $.60; children 2–12, $.30. Talking storybooks—recorded talks on animals. Keys to play records $.50 at all service stands.

Children's Facilities: Children's Zoo open Easter to mid-November, 10:30 to half hour before zoo closes. Children 1–14, $.25. Persons over 14 years, $.25. Adults must be accompanied by children. Camel, donkey cart, and pony rides $.20. Tractor trains used at 1939 New York World's Fair carry children and adults from Boston Road gate to main exhibits, $.15 each way. Bronxdale Parking field to main exhibits and return, $.10 each way.

The New York Zoological Park is the largest zoo in America. It houses some of the rarest specimens seen anywhere, some almost extinct, some common, their counterparts still roaming the wilds of Africa and Asia. Some are in cages, some in fenced-in plots.

The Aquatic Bird House, near the Fordham entrance, groups its inhabitants by their natural environments: Birds of the Treetops, Riverbanks, Tropical Lagoons, Jungle Streams, the Shore, Sea Cliffs, Marsh, Indian Pond, African Pond, and Swamp.

The Shore Birds setting looks much like Fire Island, Staten Island, or Jones Beach, with black terns, wood sandpipers, and other beach birds common to the New York area. The exhibit is completed by a hi-fi recording of wind and waves. A map on the wall opposite the ex-

An American bison ruminates.

hibit shows where these birds may be observed within a short distance from New York City.

Outside the Aquatic Bird House are a number of fenced-in bird sanctuaries. The Birdwalk is a huge cage the size of a basketball court; it houses a variety of gulls, ducks, pigeons, herons, partridges, cape teals, pelicans, pochards, and swamp hens.

248 |

Near the main entrance is the National Collection of Heads and Horns building, "in memory of the vanishing Big Game of the World." Some of the rare wild animal heads were donated by Theodore Roosevelt.

An okapi.

PART ZEBR

NO. The Ol
stripes and
Zebra's evol
independen
but serve t
same functio
concealmen
The stripes, so conspicuc
here in the open, brea
up the Okapi's outlir
in patchy forest ligh
This is an example o

The Monkey House is a perennially popular attraction. Across the grass mall are the sea-lion pool, lion house, and zebras. This area is usually crowded with children on their way to the Children's Zoo, the animal rides, and the elephant, rhino, and hippo enclosures.

The Reptile House, in the center of the zoo, is the most visited exhibit. In the nearby hall of small mammals and the Red Light Room, which simulates nighttime, are the dog-faced bat, yellow-throated

A camel gives rides to children.

Flamingoes in dazzling plumage.

marten, rusty-spotted genet, fennecs, and the Hoffmann's two-toed sloth.

Near the ape and gorilla cages are the wild sheep, ostriches, and giant Galápagos tortoises, which are now almost extinct.

Toward the Crotona entrance are the black bucks, kangaroos, wild swine, and giraffes. Near the Buffalo entrance are the llamas, yaks, bison, gazelles, and the extraordinary African Plains area, a moated enclosure much like the real plains of Africa, where antelope, lions and their cubs, deer, and birds of the wild all live together in an impressive display.

BARTOW–PELL MANSION

Address: Shore Road, Pelham Bay Park, Bronx, N.Y.
Phone: TT 5-1461

Days: Open Tuesday, Friday, and Sunday, 1–5.
Admission: $.25. Children free when accompanied by adult.

Subway: IRT Lexington Ave. (Pelham Bay Park) to last stop. Bus
to Split Rock Golf Club, Memorial Day to Labor Day.
Auto: FDR (East River) Drive, Willis Ave. Bridge, to Bruckner
Blvd., Hutchinson River Pkwy. to Orchard Beach exit. At Orchard
Beach traffic circle follow north along Shore Road. Mansion is
across from the Split Rock golf course, its entrance marked by a
gate and small plaque.

The Bartow–Pell Mansion in Pelham Bay Park easily ranks as one
of the most beautiful spots in all New York. It is so untouched by
the crowds usually found in the city's public places that one fears
to publicize its beauty.

The landscaped grounds, the immaculately manicured gardens,
the beautiful flower beds, the wide vista of Long Island Sound, the
stately architecture, the serene terrace with its wrought-iron chairs
and tables capture the ambiance of a European château more than
anything on view in New York. It is a miniature Versailles, Schön-
brunn, and Villa Borghese all wrapped into one. Life as it must
have been in a Bronx with quiet woods, dirt footpaths, flowing streams,
singing birds, and open meadows is re-created here.

On November 14, 1654, Thomas Pell obtained 9,000 acres of
land from the Sewanoe Indians. Pell, an Englishman, swore allegiance
to the Dutch of New Amsterdam and ruled as lord of the manor
at Pelham. Undoubtedly he was pleased when the English captured
the Dutch colony. On October 6, 1666, Pell was granted a royal
patent from the Duke of York.

The original manor house is said to have burned to the ground.
In 1836, Robert Bartow, descendant of the original Pell and Bartow
families, acquired the property. The present mansion was built some
time between 1836 and 1842. Its architect is unkown. The windows
and the classic recesses on the garden side of the stone house indicate
Italian inspiration. The conventional front may indicate Georgian
influence, while the interior detail is definitely Greek Revival.

In the entry hall a beautiful elliptical stairway indicates the ex-

Bartow–Pell Mansion.

tremely sophisticated taste of the builder, and the double drawing room and dining room, separated by two sliding doors, exemplify Greek Revival at its best. These rooms, though larger, are similar to the parlor-floor rooms in the Old Merchant's House in lower Manhattan. Here the pilasters are Corinthian, and the pediments over the windows and doors are decorated with carved eagles and winged cherubs.

The sitting room, library, hall dining room, and the bedrooms on the upper floors are all superbly furnished with canopied sleigh beds, pillar-and-scroll mantel clocks, Sheraton convex mirrors, and Aubusson carpets. The rooms reflect the good advice and guidance of authorities on the period. Some of the furnishings are on loan from the city's museums.

Credit for the restoration of the mansion and the care of its lovely Sunken Garden and grounds can be attributed to the 400 members of the International Garden Club and to Mrs. Charles Frederick Hoffman, who founded the club in 1914. The mansion has been the club's headquarters since that time. For two summers while he was mayor, Fiorello H. La Guardia lived here.

The Sunken Garden behind the house is surrounded by a high wall

An Empire bedroom.

254

of native stone. A series of steps leads from the terrace down to the garden, where there is a pool surrounded by formal beds of tulips and roses. Three gates of hand-wrought iron lead from the garden to the woods beyond, to the waters of Long Island Sound, and to a walk, bordered by rhododendron and ivy, that slopes to a small cemetery where the descendants of Thomas Pell are buried.

THE LONG ISLAND HISTORICAL SOCIETY

Address: 128 Pierrepont St., Brooklyn, N.Y.
Phone: MA 4-0890

Days: Open Tuesdays through Saturdays, 9–5. Closed Sundays, Mondays, national holidays, and month of August.
Admission: Free.

Subway: IRT Broadway-7th Ave. to Borough Hall or Clark St. station.
Auto: FDR (East River) Drive south to Brooklyn Bridge, Fulton St. exit. Left at Fulton, right at Montague, right again at Clinton to Pierrepont. Metered street parking.

Membership: The society welcomes as members those who wish to do research in local or family history and wish to further its purposes. Privileges include personal access to library materials, receipt of publications, etc.

Children's Facilities: A Children's History Room is open to elementary-school classes. Arrangements must be made in advance of visit.

The Long Island Historical Society is in Brooklyn Heights at the western tip of Long Island. The society, founded in 1863, is a private historical library serving its members as an archive for material related to Long Island. Although the public is allowed access to the building, one must be a fully qualified, elected member in order to use the precious historical records and collections.

The library on the second floor has a twenty-foot balcony, supported by spindly-looking wooden posts, that surrounds almost the entire floor. It looks like a picturesque version of a Civil War era bookstore. The library floor is the only section open to the general public. There is usually an exhibit of relics from the society's collections on display.

A wide selection of periodicals covers regional, state, and local his-

Long Island Historical Society.

tory with such titles as *New York Folklore, Nassau County Historical Society Journal, Newsletter from the Society for the Preservation of Long Island Antiques, New York Genealogical and Biographical Record, Long Island Forum,* etc.

The society welcomes books of any kind published about or in Brooklyn and Long Island: church and club histories; diaries, letters, directories; family records, genealogies; legal documents; property maps; early business account books; early broadsides, and sheet music. It is also interested in medals, guns, and swords owned by natives of the area; newspaper clippings; portrait paintings, drawings, lithographs, and photographs of people, places, objects, and events related to Long Island. The society also has on file microfilms of Federal census records of Long Island from 1790 to 1880.

THE BROOKLYN CHILDREN'S MUSEUM

Address: Brooklyn Ave. and Park Place, Brooklyn, N.Y.
Phone: PR 4-2900

Days: Daily, 10–5; Sundays and holidays, 1–5. Closed Sundays in July and August.
Admission: Free. (*The museum is closed temporarily.*)

Subway: (1) IRT 7th Ave. New Lots train to Kingston Ave. station. Walk 4 blocks north to Park Place. (2) IRT Lexington Ave. to Atlantic Ave. station. Cross platform and take 7th Ave. New Lots train to Kingston Ave. station. (3) IND 8th Ave. "A" train to Kingston-Throop (7 blocks to museum).
Auto: Bowery to Manhattan Bridge. Continue on Flatbush Ave. to Atlantic Ave. Left at Atlantic. Continue to Brooklyn Ave. Left to Park Place. Ample street parking.

Restaurant: Lunch room available in museum for picnic parties. Ice cream, soda available.

Gift Shop: Hobby supplies, books, toys at sales desk.

Special Events: "Schedule of Events," for $1.00 annual subscription, lists out-of-school activities, film programs, Saturday programs, pet shows, etc.

Membership: $10 annually, no special privileges.

Lectures: Saturday programs include planetarium shows, films, gallery talks, demonstrations, story hours, live-animal program. Teaching aids available on request.

The museum's main function is that of enriching the school curriculum. In winter or summer one may see half a dozen groups in the galleries getting instruction in Indian lore, on minerals, birds, or the stars.

One interesting exhibit houses a display of birds—perching birds, shore birds, pecking birds, wading and diving birds, scratching birds, swimming birds, and birds of prey all arranged in simple-to-understand showcases.

A group of rare dolls shows the traditional dress of people of the French provinces; there are also primitive prune-face and apple-face dolls made on the American frontier out of cloth, corn husks, dried

Brooklyn Children's Museum.

Two very young visitors are engrossed.

prunes, and dried apples. There are German wax dolls, a Japanese empress doll of the imperial court of the seventeenth century, and Limoges walking dolls.

A Live Animal Room contains a flying squirrel, silver fox, monkey, ring-necked doves, honey bear, a gopher, snake, skunk, guinea pig, a mouse, and opossum, all for the pleasure of small children.

The Brower Park Building is a rambling Victorian mansion house with water fountains. The Mineral Room has samples of rock and crystal, and in the entrance hall is a totem pole carved by a Brooklyn resident who came from Alaska. His Eskimo name is Geedowdosta; in Brooklyn, he is called Amos Wallace. Exhibits and dioramas on the lower floor show a solar battery that converts the sun's rays into usable electricity. Listening to the beep of the Vanguard Space Vehicle | 259 or talking into a telephone that plays back one's voice gives each child a chance to participate. The success of the museum is due to the belief that children learn by doing as well as watching.

Most of the upper floor is devoted to the Plains Indians, with displays of beads, pouches, war clubs, peace pipes, scalp locks, war bonnets, dance shields, bone breastplates, and necklaces of buffalo teeth. The buffalo sustained the Plains Indians, and hunting was their way of life. Buffalo flesh gave food, their hides made shelters, clothing, tools, and hunting gear. These Indians hunted with bows and arrows made of bone, stone, and iron. The bows were so powerful that at short range an arrow could pass entirely through a buffalo. A complete display documents the hunt and capture of a buffalo.

The Edward B. Shallow American History Room contains a series of dioramas depicting the Eskimos, Indians, Colonial settlers, and Revolutionary scenes showing the growth of the United States.

A very extensive expansion and modernization program for the museum, including the construction of a new wing, began in 1967 and is expected to take at least a year. Call museum before visiting.

PROSPECT PARK ZOO
Address: Flatbush Ave. near Empire Blvd., Brooklyn, N.Y.
Phone: SO 8-2300, ext. 2

Days: Open daily, 8–dusk. Bulidings open, 11–5.
Admission: Free.

Subway: BMT Brighton Beach to Prospect Park station.
Auto: Bowery to Manhattan Bridge, continue on Flatbush Ave. to Grand Army Plaza, then Flatbush Ave. to Prospect Park Zoo. Ample street parking.

Restaurant: Restaurant with outdoor cafe at left of entrance has light lunch, snacks. Picnic tables at right of entrance stairways.

Feeding Times:

Bird House	11
Sea-Lion Pool	1
Monkeys	1:30
Lions	2
Bear Den	2:30
Elephants	3:30
Buffalo and Zebra	4

260

Children's Facilities: Pony cart rides $.15.

At the Prospect Park Zoo spacious moated enclosures, about the width of a two-lane highway, for the Chapman zebras, Tibetan yak, elephants, and elks, provide an excellent perspective for animal-watching. Various kinds of bears amble about large boulder-strewn slopes. The generous space allotted to these animals compensates for the rather modest selection of hoofed stock and wild beasts.

Characteristic of this zoo are the droves of tagged preteens from day camps, private and public schools, YMCA's and community centers from all over Brooklyn who are shepherded from cage to cage by their counselors or teachers, who point out and try above the din to explain about the kinkajou, black leopards, the ocelot, and the civet cat.

A sea-lion pool is at the center of the zoo. The animal houses and the moated enclosures extend around the pool and to either

Relaxation at Prospect Park Zoo.

side. Within reasonable walking distance from the zoo are the Lefferts Homestead, Brooklyn Botanic Garden, and the Brooklyn Museum.

THE LEFFERTS HOMESTEAD
Address: Flatbush Ave. near Empire Blvd., Brooklyn, N.Y.
Phone: SO 8-2300, ext. 2

Days: Wednesday, Friday, Saturday, and Sunday, 1–5, except 2nd Saturday of month from November to May inclusive.
Admission: Free.

Subway: BMT Brighton Beach train to Prospect Park station.
Auto: Bowery to Manhattan Bridge, continue on Flatbush Ave. to Grand Army Plaza. Homestead is several yards past main Prospect Park Zoo entrance. Ample street parking.

The Lefferts Homestead was at one time the most northerly dwelling in Flatbush. On August 23, 1776, the family abandoned the house to escape the anticipated invasion of Kings County by the British. During the Battle of Long Island that followed, the house was destroyed.

When the Lefferts family returned, they salvaged the lumber and hardware, and in 1777 erected the present homestead. Judge John Lefferts had inherited the farm from his father, Peter, the son of Pieterse Lefferts who arrived in the New Netherlands colony in 1660 from northern Holland with his parents. Pieterse Lefferts settled in Flatbush in 1675.

The Lefferts Homestead is a notable example of Dutch Colonial style. Like the Dyckman House in upper Manhattan, it has a steeply pitched gambrel roof, accentuated by three dormers and a deep overhang supported by slender columns. The paneled front door with its small paned-glass side windows, hall wall moldings, fine archway, and banister are of particular interest.

Downstairs are the library, dining room, tea room, and a back parlor containing a pre-Revolutionary sword, a Dutch table of 1661 vintage, and the familiar Gilbert Stuart portrait of Washington. In the tea room are a Hepplewhite sofa, a Pembroke table, mahogany grandfather clock, a family Bible under glass, dated July 29, 1637, and two colored lithographs of early New York.

The library and dining room contain a flax wheel, a Hepplewhite dropleaf table, a Queen Anne lowboy, a Chippendale highboy, rush-seated side chairs and a wing chair from a house in Kent.

The Lefferts Homestead.

On the upper floor the southwest bedroom has a quilting frame, hackle for combing flax, and an early Franklin stove. A sleigh bed and several Dutch Bibles are in the northwest bedroom. Other bedrooms have dolls and "playthings of early America." In the hall cupboard are some pieces of china used by Nathan Hale's brother Enoch.

Descendants of the family presented the Homestead to the city in 1918. It was moved to Prospect Park from its original location on Flatbush Avenue.

BROOKLYN BOTANIC GARDEN AND ARBORETUM
Address: 1000 Washington Ave., Brooklyn, N.Y.
Phone: MA 2-4433

Days: Grounds open daily, 8 to sunset; from 11 on Saturdays, Sundays, and holidays. Greenhouses open daily, 10–4; Saturdays, Sundays, and holidays, 11–4:30.
Admission: Free. Ryoanji Rock Garden, $.25; greenhouses, $.10 on Saturdays, Sundays, and holidays.

Subway: (1) IRT Lexington Ave. to Atlantic Ave., cross platform to 7th Ave. train to Eastern Pkwy.-Brooklyn Museum station. (2) IRT 7th Ave. New Lots Ave. or Flatbush Ave. train to Eastern Pkwy.-Brooklyn Museum station.
Auto: Bowery to Manhattan Bridge, continue on Flatbush Ave. to Grand Army Plaza, left at Eastern Pkwy. Right onto Washington Ave. and Gardens. Ample street parking.

Gift Shop: Modest gift shop with horticultural publications in Administration Building.

Bloom Periods:

March 15–30	Crocus
April 1–15	Forsythia, Magnolias
April	Daffodils
April 1–May 10	Cherries, Crabapples
April–June	Rock Garden
May 1–15	Azaleas, Lilacs, Wisteria
May 15–30	Peonies
May–June	Iris
June–November	Roses

July–September	Lotus, Water Lillies
July–November	Annuals
September–November	Chrysanthemums
Spring–Fall	Wildflowers

Membership: $10.00 annually. Members receive announcements of popular classes, handbooks, "plant dividends."

Library: 50,000 volumes on horticultural subjects.

Children: Shakespeare Garden for children over 9 to cultivate vegetables and flowers mentioned in Shakespeare.

The Botanic Garden, on fifty acres, is almost in the center of Brooklyn. It contains a magnificent selection of familiar and exotic flora set in myriad small gardens, including the Herb Garden, Ryoanji Rock Garden, Fragrance Garden, Japanese Garden, Wildflower, Cherry Esplanade, Children's Shakespeare Garden. The grounds are well kept, and guards patrol the walks on motor scooters.

The garden is really part of the 526-acre complex of Prospect Park,

The main greenhouse at the Brooklyn Botanic Garden.

A view of the Japanese Garden.

which also includes the Brooklyn Public Library, Soldiers and Sailors Memorial Arch at Grand Army Plaza, Lefferts Homestead, the zoo, picnic grounds, horseback-riding trails, tennis courts, baseball diamonds, a lake, and the famous parade grounds.

Picnicking is not allowed; one may not walk or sit on the grass; and there are few benches. Even small canvas campstools are forbidden. Older persons unable to walk long distances may find this discouraging.

The conservatories, to the left of the Washington Avenue entrance, have a charming Victorian atmosphere. The main greenhouse houses a tropical forest of sugar cane, pineapple, bamboo, New Zealand flax, and cassia-bark trees from China, a variety that produces 85 percent of the cinnamon used in the United States. There are also the soursop, banana, avocado, Chinese fan palm, and the Panama-hat plant, a native of Peru. The trumpet tree is characterized by a completely hollow trunk and branches that, in Brazil, are inhabited by ants. The sapadilla tree is the main source of chicle. Fruits of this species are a tropical delicacy. The brown fruit, about the size of an apple, is actually a berry.

Another greenhouse contains ferns, which are found in almost every part of the world, and range in size from a few inches to the eighty-foot tree ferns of the tropics.

The Botanic Garden's famous collection of miniature Japanese bonsai trees is housed in a special hothouse. They range in age from two years to about one hundred years, and from a couple of inches to no more than two feet in height. One three-inch trident maple is more than eighty years old. A dwarf oak is well over one hundred. By severe pruning of roots and branches, and training by wire, interesting shapes and dwarf sizes can be sustained for decades. The Botanic Garden offers a course for those interested in learning the art of the bonsai tree.

The cycad greenhouse simulates great forests of 100 million years

A Japanese bonsai tree.

A replica of the Ryoanji Temple Stone Garden.

ago. The garden now has nine types of cycads growing. These trees form the link between ferns and cone-bearing forms. Many species have a thick, unbranched columnar trunk that bears a crown of large leathery pinnate leaves.

Charts in the greenhouse show major plant groups as they appeared on earth, with algae, fungi, liverworts, and mosses appearing about a billion years ago; ferns and horsetails about 300 million years ago; cycads about 200 million years ago; other conifers (pine, fir, spruce) about 100 million years ago; and flowers and grasses a mere 55 million years ago. Cycads are the most primitive living seed plants. Some cycad seeds are rich in starch, and are used as food by natives of the tropics. Cycads are commonly used for altar decorations at Eastertime.

The Garden of Fragrance to the right of the conservatories is designed for the blind, and has garlic, marjoram, lavender, peppermint, spearmint, Roman wormwood, and a variety of plants to which one's nostrils and fingers are sensitive. Signs describing the plants are in braille. The only other garden like this in the United States is in Los Angeles.

There are three types of gardens in Japan: hill-and-pond style, tea garden, and the flat style. The flat style is typified here by the Ryoanji Temple Stone Garden. Tea gardens are small, simple, unimposing gardens attached to teahouses, and may be identified by stepping-stones, paved paths, stone water basins, and stone lanterns.

The Botanic Japanese Garden is in the hill-and-pond style, intended for boating, viewing, or strolling. Architectural features are the pavilions, lanterns, and shrines. The Japanese have refined this style by the use of "borrowed scenery": gardens were so placed that the features of the terrain served as panoramic backdrops to the overall effect.

On entering the garden from the "pavilion," one looks across a lagoon to an imposing torii, which forms a decorative gateway, or portal, in Japan, where it is commonly found at the entrance to Shinto temples. The torii consists of two upright wooden posts connected at the top by two horizontal crosspieces. Torii are frequently reproduced on Japanese travel posters.

Directly behind the torii is the Religious Shrine, typical of the traditional Shinto shrines in Japan. This one is dedicated to "Inari," the God of Harvest, and Protector of Plants. In Japan such shrines are seen along the streets and in or near private estates. Woods used in this shrine are white cedar, ash, redwood, and cypress, and the shrine is held together by wooden pegs.

Behind the Japanese Garden are the crabapples and the Cherry Esplanade, probably one of the most beautiful scenes in New York at cherry-blossom time. Beyond the esplanade are the Armistice Maples, planted on November 11, 1918. They have become huge

Within a grove of trees.

shade trees. The walks around the esplanade have benches.

The Cranford Rose Garden is particularly noted for its hybrid tea roses of infinite variety, with such evocative names as Captain Fain Bold, First Love, Gracious Lady, Rochefort, Suntan, Oklahoma, and Opera.

At the southern end of the Botanic Garden is the Ryoanji Temple Stone Garden, a replica of the five-hundred-year-old original in Kyoto. The garden has no trees or bushes, and is about the size of a tennis court. It is paved with finely crushed stone, arranged in straight and slightly curving rows, like new plantings on a farm or like ripples from a stone thrown into a quiet lake. Among the rows are arranged groups of rocks. This beautiful and most unusual garden is a marvelous pool of peace and calm in our great city and should not be missed.

BROOKLYN MUSEUM
Address: Eastern Pkwy. at Washington Ave., Brooklyn, N.Y.
Phone: NE 8-5000

Days: Mondays through Saturdays, 10–5; Sundays and holidays, 1–5.
Admission: Free.

Subway: (1) IRT Lexington Ave. to Atlantic Ave. station. Cross platform to 7th Ave. train to Eastern Pkwy.-Brooklyn Museum station. (2) IRT 7th Ave. New Lots or Flatbush Ave. train to Eastern Pkwy.-Brooklyn Museum station.
Auto: Bowery to Manhattan Bridge to Flatbush Ave. Continue on Flatbush Ave. to Grand Army Plaza. Follow Eastern Pkwy. signs around traffic circle. Continue on Eastern Pkwy. to Museum, on right. Metered parking in front of building. Public parking lot at rear of building. $.25 fee for first hour, $.10 each additional hour.

Restaurant: Museum cafeteria, first floor rear, has hot lunches, snacks, tea. Open Mondays to Saturdays, 10–4:30. Sundays and holidays, 1–4:30.

Gift Shop: Exceptional collection of handicrafts for sale. See description below. Museum publications and paperbacks are also available.

Special Events: Sunday-afternoon concerts in Sculpture Court, gallery talks, special exhibitions, movies.

Membership: $10.00 up. Membership privileges include lecture course discounts, etc. Junior memberships free.

Library and Research: Art reference library, closed July and August. Open Mondays to Fridays, 1–5.

Lectures: Background Hour Lectures for school classes.

Children's Facilities: Children's concerts, art classes, excursions; junior members' programs include clubs, subscription to *Junior Bulletin*, etc. Junior Aide program enlists young volunteers to work in the museum.

If you were sitting on the back of a burro climbing the Andes of Peru, and you passed a large group of men and women, you might well ask where they came from. The answer could be: "The Brooklyn Museum." If you were out driving in Connecticut on a Sunday afternoon and flipped the radio dial to a concert, you might well wonder where the music came from. The announcer might answer just at

The Brooklyn Museum.

*Totempoles in
the Hall of the Americas.*

that time: "The Brooklyn Museum." And if you took a Staten Island bus and encountered a group of teen-agers on their way to dig for Colonial artifacts, you wouldn't have to ask where they were from; you would already know. These are just a few examples of the many activities the Brooklyn Museum is engaged in.

The diverse activities, programs, and services of the Brooklyn Museum include visits to historic houses and museums, seminars on art, museum treasure hunts for young members, dance programs, films, children's art classes, an art reference library, Community Committee's "Museum on Wheels," a Fashion and Design Laboratory, Conservation Laboratory (where paintings are cleaned by ultrasonic apparatus),

A raven mask from the South Seas.

and a vast art training program. The Museum Art School has a separate entrance, at the right wing of the building, and offers courses in painting, drawing, sculpture, and ceramics. It also provides a number of scholarships.

The original building was designed by the famous architectural firm of McKim, Mead & White. Since its construction in 1897, a number of revisions have been made, of course. A monumental front staircase once led to the present third floor, and without the stairs the first-floor entrance looks somewhat out of proportion to the rest of the façade. The museum, along with the Botanical Garden, Lefferts Homestead, the public library, and Prospect Park Zoo, completes Brooklyn's major cultural center.

The museum is conceived as a place for enjoyment, recreation, and education, not as an institution where art is kept remote from the common man. The museum's success as one of the major cultural forces in New York is measured, not by attendance, but by an "individual's recollection of what was seen, what was thought, and what was felt."

There are five floors of exhibition space. The first floor is the special exhibition area. Its galleries are devoted to the arts of the primitive peoples of Africa, pre-Columbian Central and South America, North American Indians, Oceania, South Seas, and the Ainu. There is an outside garden devoted to sandstone and brownstone "tenement sculpture" of the 1890-1910 period, collected by the Anonymous Arts Recovery Society. The society is composed of enterprising art scholars who have made great efforts to recover keystone sculpture and reliefs from the hands of demolition crews. Carved ornaments of this type still adorn many Lower East Side tenements. Gargoyles, limestone flowers and beasts, columns and pediments in the garden are all from demolished buildings. They are good examples of the art of stonemasonry. The first floor also contains the cafeteria and Gallery Shop.

The Gallery Shop sells folk art from over sixty countries. It is the only museum shop with an exhibition program featuring original arts and crafts of high quality sold at reasonable prices. For $.05 you can buy hand-colored animal plants from France, or for $30 you can buy a silver necklace from Pakistan. Some of the other handicrafts are exotic bud vases from Israel, traditional toys from Japan, miniature Chinese wood carvings, ceramic bulls from Peru, costume dolls from Italy, Polish painted roosters, Zuni ceramic owls from New Mexico, paper puppet cutouts from Greece, shell animals, palm buttons, jumping jacks, glass dragons, feather birds, and toy friction bugs. The Gallery Shop most appropriately leads into the gallery of primitive arts.

The entrance room has thirty-two glass cases, each of which contains a weapon (spear, machete, hatchet, bow) and a piece of woven textile. The two objects in each case represent what is attributed to the men and what to the women of a tribe. The tribes are those of the Pacific Islands, Africa, and the Americas. Each exhibit clearly reveals the specific qualities, materials, and techniques of each culture and the direct relation of arts and crafts to daily life. Each culture has produced objects that are useful and beautiful. The Brooklyn Museum was among the first institutions in the United States to collect the native arts of Africa, Oceania, and Indian America. Even before the turn of the century, museum expeditions were sent to all parts of the

Jolyon Hofsted teaching ceramics.

world to document and assemble the sculpture, ornaments, costumes, and crafts of the cultures exhibited here.

To the right are the crafts of the Pacific Islands, with ceremonial shields, boomerangs, drums covered with lizard skins, face masks, and a variety of betel-nut crushers. The "Art of Africa" display has spears, ceremonial masks in the form of hideous creatures, antelope, buffalo, secret-society and initiation masks, fetishes, male and female figures, ceremonial shields of bamboo and mahogany, and wooden doors with allegorical motifs.

Dominating the Hall of the Americas are five magnificent ceiling-high totem poles. Carvings of mythological animals and figures represent the ancestral crests of the families that owned the houses in front of which the totems were placed. Four huge cases in the Great Hall of the museum present a comprehensive picture of the colorful arts of Indian peoples from the Arctic to the Argentine. With the last vestiges of Indian life in the Americas disappearing, this collection constitutes a unique source of information. One section displays the art of the ancient and modern Eskimo, including spirit masks, carved ivory, kayaks, and outerwear made from the skins of seal and caribou.

In the area devoted to the Northwest Coast tribes, mythical and ceremonial objects include grotesque man-like figures that are particularly fearsome. An electrically operated straw-covered raven mask clicks its beak up and down in the darkened case. A thunderbird mask represents a mythical creature whose flapping wings made thunder while his flashing eyes made lightning. On exhibit also are unique examples of Central Andean weaving, painted cloth, tapestry pouches, fringed robes, silver, pottery, feather caps, burial urns, jewelry, and effigy jars.

The Nathan Sturges Jarvis Collection on the Plains Indians contains some of the oldest and historically most important pieces in existence: bone chest ornaments, carved pipes, decorated buckskin shirts and robes, feather war bonnets, moccasins, snowshoes, and implements of war. This material, unique because of its age and documentation, was collected by Dr. Jarvis while he was an army surgeon at Fort Snelling, Minnesota, between 1833 and 1836. Specimens comparable to this collection that are in other museums are generally without documentation.

The second floor houses the William A. Putnam Memorial Print Room, Edward C. Blum Design Laboratory, American and European print collections, and the arts of the East: China, Japan, India, Thailand, Persia.

*"Holy Wisdom," a limestone lunette from Egypt
of the Coptic period, 5th century* A.D.

The collections of the Edward C. Blum Design Laboratory have
traveled all over the world, as well as to design schools throughout
the country. Much has been shown on both films and television. In one
year the laboratory staged nearly fifteen public exhibitions.

The William A. Putnam Memorial Print Room (open by appointment) has 20,000 prints and drawings from the late fourteenth century
to those of the most contemporary artists, with particular emphasis on
German Expressionists. From this collection come the exhibitions on
this floor. Individual monographs on contemporary Americans are
compiled, prepared, and published here.

| 277

Also sharing the floor are the exhibits of "Arts of Islam and the
Indian East." Various types of glazed, lustered, and painted ceramics
are shown. Indian miniature painting (Rajput) and Islamic rugs are
also here. In the center of the gallery is a Jain Rest Home, with carved

George Washington by Gilbert Stuart, 1796.

pillars and door and walls all covered with Golconda cotton panels. The home, about six by eight feet, was a room attached to temples for the convenience of worshipers.

A large part of the second-floor gallery is devoted to Oriental arts of the Han, T'ang, Chou, Yin, Ming, and Ch'ing dynasties. Many centuries of civilization and religious transition are represented. The Oriental collections indicate a more complicated social organization and a wider range and sublety of form and subject than the collections on the first floor.

The third floor contains Coptic arts, Egyptian, Greek, and Roman art, art of the Near East, the Lecture Hall, the Auditorium, and the Wilbour Library of Egyptology, which ranks among the finest in the world.

The Hagop Kevorkian Gallery of the Ancient Middle East consists of twelve Assyrian reliefs of gypseous alabaster taken from the royal city of Kalhu. In the wing to the left are works of the Ramessid, Roman, Ptolemaic, and Late periods of Egypt. At the very end of the gallery is the portrait of an Egyptian official. It is of the late Ptolemaic period, and ranks among the best portraits from the Nile Valley before Roman domination. It is now possible for visitors to rent Acoustiguide tours of the Egyptian galleries that have been taped by the curator Bernard Bothner and his assistant Jean Keith.

The section on predynastic and early dynastic Egypt contains early Egyptian sculpture. The pottery figures date from 4000 B.C., and include female figures with birdlike heads, with arms outstretched, possibly engaged in ritual dances. A rare representation in black granite of a female sphinx made circa 1900 B.C., is considered one of the great examples of Egyptian Middle Kingdom sculpture.

The gallery surrounding the auditorium has works of Coptic Egypt, an era when Christianity was replacing paganism. The Copts tended to draw on classical mythology for art subjects. Architectural reliefs and elaborately woven fabrics were major accomplishments of the period.

The fourth floor holds American and European costume collections, objects of pewter, silver, ceramics, glass, and twenty-five completely furnished Early American interiors, of the period 1715 through 1880, from New England, the South, New York, and New Jersey.

In the central gallery the Jan Martense Schenck House, a clapboard farmhouse with Dutch doors built in 1675, has been reconstructed beam by beam. The house is an example of seventeenth-century Brooklyn architecture, and was formerly at 2133 East 63rd Street. The only surviving inhabited Dutch cottage of that era in Brooklyn is the Pieter Claesen Wycoff House, at Claredon Road and East 59th Street. Built in 1637, it is now in a sadly dilapidated condition. It is the oldest occupied frame house in the United States.

Silver, ceramics, pewter, glass, Bennington pottery, American samplers, and the Furniture Gallery take up the remainder of this central area. The remainder of the fourth floor is devoted to room settings from American homes of the Victorian, Colonial, and early Republican periods. The rooms are arranged in subway-tunnel fashion, and appear gloomy because of the poor illumination and extra walls, which recreate the actual enclosures but hinder the view of the rooms and their furnishings. The parlors, bedrooms, dining rooms, and kitchens are carefully detailed, as in the James Perry Plantation, built in 1806 near Summerville, North Carolina.

Representing the Victorian era is a sitting room from the John D. Rockefeller four-story brownstone that stood on West 54th Street in Manhattan. This is a vivid example of home decoration around 1884, when tastes ran to exotic Moorish tiles, gold-brocaded walls, ebony and oak panels, decorated ceilings, plush velvet, and candelabra.

The fifth floor and mezzanine house collections of American and

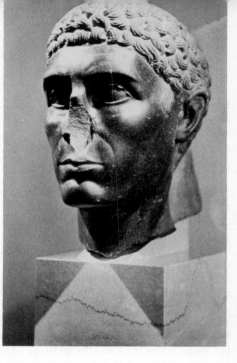

An Egyptian official of the Ptolemaic period about 60 B.C.

European paintings, sculpture, watercolors, medieval and Renaissance art. A huge, crudely fashioned ancient Spanish door leads to the European collections. More than a thousand paintings at the Brooklyn Museum which were inaccessible to the public have just made their appearance for the first time in a novel method of display. The Open Study Storage Gallery, as the museum calls its new project, now offers its panorama of paintings on a series of rotating and sliding panels, a method of display that is used by large commercial galleries.

The Department of Painting and Sculpture usually presents an exhibition from one major private collection each year. There have been exhibitions of the Nelson Rockefeller, Louis E. Stern, Hirshhorn Foundation, and the Herbert A. Goldstone collections. This special exhibition program exists primarily to create, develop, and reward aesthetic perception.

The American Collection traces American painting from the Colonial period. The museum has built a comprehensive collection of Colonial portraits. The Federal Period is identified with Benjamin West, the first American to go abroad to study art, and around whom

A sculpture in the Frieda Schiff Warburg Garden of works collected by the Anonymous Arts Recovery Society.

a school developed. Thomas Sully, Charles Wilson Peale, Ralph Earle, and Gilbert Stuart were his best-known disciples. Stuart's portrait of Washington is a prime example of the excellence of early portraiture.

The Hudson River School of painting is represented by a number of pastoral scenes depicting the wonders of our national landscape in a romantic glorification of nature. Other sections of the American Collection are devoted to paintings by "The Eight," Social Realists, prewar and postwar Abstract Expressionists and Impressionists. The fifth-floor mezzanine displays a sizable collection of watercolors by John Singer Sargent, Winslow Homer, and other American and European artists.

NEW YORK AQUARIUM

Address: Coney Island, Brooklyn, N.Y.
Phone: CO 6-8500

Days: Open daily, 10–10 in summer; 10–5 in winter. Open all holidays.
Admission: Adults $.90, children 5–16, $.45. Special group rates must be prearranged. Children under 5 free.

Subway: (1) IND 6th Ave. "D" train to West 8th St., Coney Island. (2) BMT Brighton train to West 8th St., Coney Island.
Auto: Brooklyn-Battery Tunnel to Gowanus Pkwy., Shore Pkwy. to Exit 10. South on Ocean Pkwy. to Surf Ave. and Aquarium. 2-hour metered parking on Surf Ave. Aquarium parking-lot fees: weekdays $.75; Saturday, $1.00; Sunday, $1.50.

Restaurant: Outdoor cafe-restaurant has light lunches, snacks, and view of beach. Picnic tables near small snack bar.

Gifts: Shop near whale tank has large stock of souvenirs in singularly bad taste. Good selection of hobby supplies, books. Guide to Aquarium is excellent.

On entering the aquarium you immediately face the underwater tanks of the beluga whales. These whales may reach 17 feet at full growth and weigh more than 4,000 pounds. They are not completely white until they are five years old. The whale tank can also be viewed from above, on the terrace.

At the tank of electric eels a demonstration is given that shows the ability of the eels to produce sufficient electricity to light bulbs, sound

Zebrafish at the New York Aquarium.

buzzers, flash strobe lights, and shoot from 375 to 550 volts into a voltmeter. These eels, which have no teeth, scales, or spines, and cannot even see very well, reach a length of nine feet.

The morays are closely related to eels, and are feared by fishermen and divers who encounter them in the crevices of coral reefs and find them savagely aggressive.

Among the other fish displayed are the hogfish, which has a nose shaded red and which, from the front, looks like a hog; the piranha, a fearsome South American species noted for its viciousness; the venomous stonefish, and the zebrafish, a member of the scorpion fish family, with thirteen spines, all believed to be venomous.

In the world's oceans there are more varieties of creatures than all the kinds of mammals, birds, and reptiles of the earth combined. The aquarium has many curious sea animals on display, including the sea anemone, with beautiful white tentacles that wave gracefully in the water; the Pacific sea cucumber, related to starfishes, which feeds on sand and mud and lives in that part of the ocean where weirdly lighted, ghostly creatures haunt the depths; one of the most graceful sights is that of the schooling fish—striped bass, herring, mackerel, dogfish, and Nova Scotia alewhite—which swim counterclockwise in unison around and around almost hypnotically while the sunlight streams down into the tank.

Baluga whales.

There are also pools of penguins, seals, and walruses on the aquarium grounds.

The setting for the New York Aquarium is a strip of beach with a boardwalk separating it from the Atlantic Ocean. The aquarium has been on this site since 1942. Previously it was in the Castle Clinton structure in Battery Park, Manhattan. The present building on twelve-acre Seaside Park plans to build additional wings. Attendance at the aquarium is about 343,000 annually.

QUEENS BOTANICAL GARDEN
Address: 43–50 Main St. at Dahlia Ave., Flushing, N.Y.
Phone: TU 6-3800

Days: Open daily, 9 to dusk.
Admission: Free.

| 285

Subway: IRT Flushing line from Times Square or Grand Central to Main St. station.

Humboldt penguins.

Auto: Queens–Midtown Tunnel to Long Island Expressway. Main St., Flushing exit north to Dahlia Ave. Ample street parking.

Membership: $3.00 to $100.00 annual membership. Members receive publication.

Lectures: Variety of lectures on horticultural subjects. Inquire in Administration Building.

The Queens Botanical Garden is the most recent addition to the botanic gardens of New York City. Because it is conveniently located in the heart of Flushing, the garden, the historic Friends Meeting House, and the Bowne House may easily be encompassed in one excursion. The garden is still in the early stages of development. Many young trees and plantings are in evidence, as well as a new administration building, completed in 1963, that appears spacious, well lighted, and cheerful. It expresses the outlook of the Botanical Society in providing expanded facilities for the Queens community. Plans for the future include two greenhouses and a fragrance garden.

Perkins Memorial Garden at the Queens Botanical Garden.

286

Some of the features of the garden are: spring flowering bulbs (narcissus and tulip); the Perkins Memorial Garden, which contains thousands of popular varieties of roses; an ericaceous garden (woody plants, shrubs, and small trees); an astor collection with twenty varieties; cold frames that protect the plants over the winter; soil-testing facilities; turf trails that demonstrate characteristics of grasses, and an arboretum of 150 evergreen trees.

To serve its community and interested visitors, the Garden Society offers a wide and interesting variety of practical lectures and demonstrations devoted to designing home gardens, flower arranging, lawn-making, pruning, care of house plants, attracting birds to a garden, fertilizers, and weedkillers. A nominal fee is charged for the lectures.

FRIENDS MEETING HOUSE
Address: 137–16 Northern Blvd., Flushing, N.Y.
Phone: RO 2-9743

Days: Sundays, 2–5. Visitors welcome at worship, Sunday at 11. When closed, out-of-town visitors may call for an appointment.
Admission: Free.

Subway: IRT Flushing line from Times Square or Grand Central to Main St. station.
Auto: Queens–Midtown Tunnel to Long Island Expressway. Main St., Flushing exit north. Right at Northern Blvd. to Meeting House. Metered street parking.

Lectures: Free guided tour of building.

It is unlikely that anyone would pass by the historic Friends Meeting House in the busy shopping center of Flushing without noticing the building. There is nothing quite like it anywhere in the city.

The Meeting House was built in 1694 on land given by John Bowne, and is one of America's oldest places of worship. It has been in continuous use, except for a period during the Revolution. British soldiers seized the property and used it variously as a prison, a hospital, and for storage of hay.

This rare specimen of Colonial architecture stands behind a low stone wall. The two-story, rectangular wooden building is distinguished for its four-sided hip roof, wooden shutters, and small-paned windows. There is an open porch across the entire front of the lower story. The

Friends Meeting House.

porch roof is supported by slender square wooden posts. The doors from the porch swing open by means of a weight on ropes and a system of pulleys. Original handmade iron door hinges, latches, and locks are still in evidence. The doors open directly into the meeting room, which has plain white plaster walls, no decorative cornices, tinted glass, or glowing fabrics. The room has simple, open-back wooden benches covered with fiber matting. All the benches face the center of the room. The overhead beams are held up by wooden posts. The corners are anchored with "ship's knees," the Colonial version of today's ell-shaped brackets.

Although the building's historical significance is assured simply by its being such a well-preserved monument of its era, it is also a memorial to the early citizens of the Flushing area who refused to persecute the Quaker settlers as ordered by the governor of their colony.

BOWNE HOUSE
Address: Bowne St. at Fox Lane, Flushing, N.Y.
Phone: FL 9-0528

Days: Tuesday, Saturday, and Sunday, 2:30–4:15.
Admission: Free.

Subway: IRT Flushing line from Times Square or Grand Central to Main St. station.
Auto: Queens–Midtown Tunnel to Long Island Expressway. Main St. Flushing exit north. Right turn at Northern Blvd. Right turn at Bowne St. to Fox Lane. Ample street parking.

The Bowne House is on a quiet side street in Flushing among the pleasant two-family houses typical of this area. Numerous oak trees shade the wide street.

The oldest part of this two-story saltbox was erected in 1661 by John Bowne on land purchased from the Indians ten years earlier. In addition to being one of the oldest buildings extant in New York, it is also considered a shrine to religious freedom.

The house is well cared for by informed guides who painstakingly explain every item on the premises. Since the caretakers sometimes close the house before the posted closing time, it is a good idea first to make a check by phone. The Bowne House, like the Van Cortlandt House in upper Manhattan, discourages children under twelve from entering, even if accompanied by adults.

The earliest section of the house is the kitchen, which has its original, pegged floors. The semicircular oven in the great fireplace could bake as many as forty pies at one time. On the mantel is a rare pewter plate with a Dutch inscription, dated 1656. There are also a rare "betty lamp" and a rushlight. A cupboard holds a set of leather drinking tankards with figures embossed in the leather. | 289

In this kitchen John Bowne expounded his Quaker philosophy, in violation of Governor Peter Stuyvesant's edict of 1657 that the religion of the Dutch Reformed Church was to be the only religion. It was

Bowne House.

forbidden for anyone in the colony to entertain a Quaker or attend a Quaker meeting. Bowne permitted illegal meetings in this house and was arrested, imprisoned, and subsequently banished to Ireland. It was his courageous commitment and determination that eventually brought freedom of assembly for the Quakers.

George Fox, founder of the Quaker faith, preached outside the house on June 7, 1672. Etchings inside the building show the Fox oaks, marking the site where he spoke. A plaque in the garden commemorates the Flushing Remonstrance, an appeal dated December 27, 1657, petitioning the governor for liberty of conscience for the Quakers.

KING MANSION

Address: 153rd St. and Jamaica Ave., Jamaica, N.Y.
Phone: OL 8-6530

Days: Monday, Wednesday, and Saturday, 1:30–4:30.
Admission: Free. Children under 14 not admitted without an adult.

Subway: 8th Ave. Queens "E" train to Parsons Blvd. station. Walk two blocks to King Park at 89th Ave. and 153rd St.
Auto: Queens–Midtown Tunnel to Long Island Expressway. To Parsons Blvd. exit to Jamaica Ave.; turn right to 153rd St. Metered street parking.

The King Mansion stands at the edge of a pleasant neighborhood park that has an old-time circular, domed, open bandstand in the center.

Rufus King purchased the estate on November 20, 1805, for $12,000; it consisted of ninety acres, extending north to the present Grand Central Parkway and east to Grace Episcopal Church. The church is on Jamaica Avenue today, just two blocks away. Its graveyard contains some extraordinary gravestones that look almost new but are as old as 1738 (such as that of Elbert Willett). The quality of the primitive angels' heads, skeletons, skull and crossbones places these early markers in the category of Early American folk art. Rufus King and dozens of his descendants are buried in the Grace Episcopal churchyard.

The Kings were one of America's leading families. Rufus King was a "carpetbagger" from Maine. Graduating from Harvard in 1777, he served as a delegate to the Continental Congress in the late 1780's, was a minister to England under Washington, Adams, and Jefferson, and became one of the first two United States senators from New York in 1789.

King Mansion.

For the short time that King himself lived in the mansion, he enjoyed the life of a gentleman farmer, continuing his correspondence from his library with the influential and prominent men of the day and entertaining in his beautiful dining room. King and his wife, Mary Alsop, reared five brilliant children: John Alsop King, governor of New York in 1856; Charles, editor of the New York *American* in 1823 and president of Columbia College; James Gore, president of the Erie Railroad and congressman from New Jersey; Edward, founder of the Cincinnati Law School; and Frederic Gore, a distinguished physician.

The mansion's barnlike appearance can be attributed to its gambrel roof. The eight-room house has three sections; the oldest, in the rear, dating from 1700, is now a storage depot for the wheelbarrows, shovels, and rakes of the city's Parks Department. At various times the house has been an inn, a farmhouse, and a parsonage for Grace Episcopal's ministers (1710–1755).

Around the turn of the century the building was acquired by the city. Because over the years it has been decorated piecemeal by volunteer workers, the furnishings have fluctuated from a time of total neglect to that of an overzealous modern decor. At one low point ugly radiators were installed. The floors in many of the rooms suffered from repeated coats of heavy-duty paint, as did the delicate wall moldings, woodwork, and even some of the furnishings. The wallpapers reflected contemporary bargain-basement prices rather than the taste of the Sheraton or Empire periods.

In 1964 an electrical fire took its toll of two rooms containing many valuable antiques. Many items were salvaged—a wall clock dated 1700, a family Bible (1637), an antique coin collection, and the Dutch Delft tiles bordering the fireplace. As a result of the fire, rehabilitation has brought authenticity to much of the contents of the mansion. New fabrics for the parlor windows, for example, are of woven silk, adapted from a design by Philippe de La Salle, a famous eighteenth-century textile manufacturer in France.

STATEN ISLAND INSTITUTE OF ARTS AND SCIENCES

Address: 75 Stuyvesant Place, Staten Island, N.Y.
Phone: SA 7-1135

Days: Daily 10–5; Sundays, 2–5. Closed Mondays and major holidays.
Admission: Free.

Subway: IRT 7th Ave. or IRT Lexington Ave. to South Ferry station; then take Staten Island Ferry (5¢) to St. George.
Bus: From St. George walk 3 blocks to Wall St. for bus.
Auto: Drive south to Battery and Staten Island Ferry. Alternate driving route via Brooklyn–Battery Tunnel, Belt Pkwy. to Verrazano–Narrows Bridge (Rt. 278). Principal attraction of bridge for Manhattan-based Staten-Island-bound motorists is avoiding the long lines at ferry. Leave Rt. 278 at Hylan Blvd. exit, continue to Bay St., past New York ferries to Richmond Terr., left at Hamilton Pl., left again at Stuyvesant Pl. Metered street parking. Those coming off ferry in St. George take scenic walk 3 blocks along Richmond Terr. and turn left at Wall St.

Special Events: Sunday concerts, nature programs, film series, lectures and demonstrations in arts and crafts.

Membership: $10.00 annually, includes subscription to monthly bulletin, art rental gallery privileges, etc.

| 293

Gift Shop: Sales counter near lobby entrance for hobby supplies, toys, books.

This two-story Colonial-style brick building has a pleasant entranceway with a semicircle of benches grouped around the front door. It is a modest museum wherein young children can see dioramas of trees and their development, conservation, seashells of the New York area, and Indian relics related to Staten Island.

One diorama asks, "Does Civilization Have to Mean: Polluted Air? Polluted Water? Littered Roadsides? Automobile Graveyards? Rubbish Everywhere?" It shows the debris of modern civilization, with beer cans, burned-out light bulbs, crushed cardboard boxes, broken toys, chunks of wood, and old newspapers lying in a heap, and thus makes its point very strongly indeed.

Another exhibit shows the remains uncovered in an Indian burial ground, many of which are now being unearthed on Staten Island because of extensive construction of roads and housing developments. The bones on view here were found in 1960 in Tottenville, south of the end of Hylan Boulevard, near the Conference House. The Indian was probably a woman about thirty-five when she died about 1200 A.D. She belongs to the late Woodland Period when people did not bury artifacts with their dead. It is thought that the arrowheads and spearheads embedded with the bones were the cause of death. Sharp oyster

Staten Island Institute.

shells set around the body were believed to have been placed there to keep away animals.

A major project of the Staten Island Museum is the High Rock Nature Conservation Center, a seventy-acre, hilly oak and hickory woodland of nature trails where Audubon buffs and conservationists can enjoy the sight of sweet gum, cherry birch, and swamp azalea. Booklets are available for self-guided walks. The entrance to High Rock is on Nevada Avenue, four blocks north of Richmond Road.

STATEN ISLAND ZOO IN BARRETT PARK
Address: 640 Broadway, West New Brighton, Staten Island, N.Y.
Phone: GI 2-3100

Days: Open daily, 10–5.
Admission: Free.

Subway: IRT 7th Ave. or IRT Lexington Ave. to South Ferry station. Take Staten Island Ferry (5¢) to St. George.
Bus: From St. George take bus #107 to Broadway.
Auto: (1) From St. George turn right on Richmond Terrace, left at Broadway to zoo. (2) From Verrazano Bridge take Clove Road exit to zoo at Broadway. Ample street parking.

Restaurant: Vending machines for soda, ice cream.

Gift Shop: Sales counter has candy, toys, hobby supplies, Zoological Society publications.

Feeding Times:

Birds	11:30
Mammals	2:30 (except Saturday)
Reptiles	3:30 (Sundays)

Library: Small reference library open to public and students.

Lectures: Staff members available only to organized groups (schoolchildren, Boy Scouts, etc.) for tours and lectures.

| 295

Publication: Staten Island Zoological Society monthly *News Bulletin.*

This modest zoo is set in an eight-acre park delightfully shaded by tall

Staten Island Zoo.

pin oaks, Norway maples, and sweet gum trees. The zoo has separate bird and mammal wings, a reptile wing of international repute, and an aquarium.

The aquarium has a fine collection of American alligators and many kinds of frogs and toads: green tree and leopard frogs, Colombian horned and bull frogs, North American tiger salamanders, and Blomberg toads.

The famous collection of reptiles includes blood pythons, boa constrictors, and one of the largest collections of rattlesnakes ever assembled anywhere—the Panamint, the Mojave, Sonora sidewinder, mottled rock, ridge-nosed, black-tailed, timber, tiger, diamond back, and midget faded. There are also the West African green mamba and the puff adder, which are among the deadliest in the world.

The bird collection includes woodpeckers, robins, concave-casqued hornbills, birds from India, Burma, Java, and the Himalayas; shiny

A Golden Eagle.

cowbirds from Argentina; a king vulture, a crowned hawk-eagle, and a golden eagle. Many of the bird enclosures simulate the natural habitats of the birds. | 297

The head of the zoo hospital is Dr. Patricia O'Connor, the only full-time woman zoo veterinarian in the United States. Her bibliography of the diseases of wild animals is well known.

FORT WADSWORTH MILITARY MUSEUM

Address: School Road and Bay St., Staten Island, N.Y.
Phone: GI 7-5100, ext. 409

Days: Saturdays, Sundays, and holidays, 1–5. Groups accommodated.
Admission: Free.

Subway: IRT 7th Ave. or IRT Lexington Ave. to South Ferry, then
take Staten Island Ferry (5¢) to St. George.
Bus: From St. George take bus #2 to School Road.
Auto: (1) From St. George left along Bay St. to Fort. (2) From Ver-
razano Bridge, exit at Hylan Blvd., then to Bay St., right to Fort.
Free parking lot.

New York's newest small museum will have a particular appeal to children who are fascinated by military history. Here are to be found the
rampart cannons, rifles, uniforms, medals, flags, and other paraphernalia that document a dozen or more wars from the Dutch-Colonial
period to Vietnam.

This museum, established in 1966 by Maj. General T. R. Yancey, is

*View of Battery Weed and Verrazano-Narrows Bridge
from the Fort Wadsworth Military Museum.*

Inside Fort Wadsworth Museum.

situated in three bays of the quadrangle in Fort Tompkins barracks built in 1847. Built on a hilltop, Fort Wadsworth affords a spectacular view of the Narrows, the Lower Bay, and the Verrazano Bridge. The abandoned Battery Weed is directly below Fort Tompkins barracks.

These fortifications have been held successively by Dutch, British, and Americans since 1663 and have guarded the southern part of New York harbor.

BILLIOU–STILLWELL–PERINE HOUSE
Address: 1476 Richmond Road, Dongan Hills, Staten Island, N.Y.
Phone: 987-7379

Days: Saturdays and Sundays, 2–5, April to November.
Admission: Adults $.25, children free.

Subway: IRT 7th Ave. or IRT Lexington Ave. to South Ferry,
  then take Staten Island Ferry (5¢) to St. George.
Bus: From St. George bus #108, #113, or #117 to Cromwell.
Auto: (1) From St. George left along Bay St., right to Victory Blvd.,
  left at St. Paul's. Continue as road name changes to Van Duzer,

then to Richmond Road. Continue to #1476. (2) From Verrazano Bridge, Richmond Road exit to house. Ample street parking.

The Billiou–Stillwell–Perine House closely resembles a European farm-house of the seventeenth century. It was built by Pierre Billiou in 1663 on property he acquired under a Dutch patent granted two years earlier. Billiou headed the first permanent settlement on Staten Island.

The rear section of the house was the original parlor-kitchen. It has a remarkable fireplace without sides that is surmounted by a great chimney supported by a framework and two columns just below the ceiling beams. This construction was typical of the Low Countries, and gives the room its Old World charm. The walls on this side of the farmhouse are composed of French or Belgian stone about 18 inches thick. Their soundproofing quality would be the envy of dwellers in contemporary thin-walled apartment houses.

In 1677, Captain Thomas Stillwell, a sheriff, magistrate, and militia captain received an English patent for the Billiou property. Stillwell had married Billiou's daughter in 1670. It is believed that Billiou

Perine House.

A welcoming hearth.

transferred the property to his son-in-law for safekeeping when he lost favor with the British.

The portion of the house facing Richmond Road was put up separately by Stillwell in 1680. The Staten Island historian Loring Mc-Mullen believes that the Stillwell portion of the house may be an old house from Oude Dorp at South Beach that was abandoned in 1679, or the house may have belonged to Thomas Stillwell, who moved and reassembled it, piece by piece, on the Billiou site. That the Stillwell side was added later is evidenced by the smaller, English-style fireplace, different casement windows, and the rafters and beams that indicate former use.

The front and back buildings are so arranged that two families could occupy the property and be independent of each other. In fact, until recently there was no doorway to connect the two houses.

In 1760, 1790, and 1830 additions were made to the house by the Perine family. The property was acquired in 1915 by the Staten Island Historical Society. The Federated Garden Clubs of New York undertook the planning and development of the formal garden at the side of the house.

JACQUES MARCHAIS CENTER OF TIBETAN ART

Address: 340 Lighthouse Ave., Staten Island, N.Y.
Phone: EL 1-3280

Days: Weekdays except Mondays, 2–5; 2nd and 4th Saturdays and
   Sundays of each month, 2–5. Closed October 31st to April 1st.
Admission: $.50.

Subway: IRT 7th Ave. or IRT Lexington Ave. to South Ferry, then
   take Staten Island Ferry (5¢) to St. George.
Bus: From St. George take bus #113 to Lighthouse Ave. Walk up hill.
Auto: (1) From St. George left along Bay St., right to Victory Blvd.,
   left at St. Paul's. Continue as road name changes to Van Duzer,
   then Richmond Road. Turn right at two stone posts marking beginning of Lighthouse Ave. Continue up hill to #340 on right.
   (2) From Verrazano Bridge take Richmond Road exit. Follow road
   to Lighthouse Ave. as above. Ample street parking.

Library: Large collection of Orientalia open to public.

The Jacques Marchais Center of Tibetan Art is on top of Lighthouse
Hill, the highest point along the eastern seaboard. The museum overlooks the woodlands and lakes of rural Staten Island. On a clear day
you can see the entire lower bay of New York in the distance.

The altar in Jacques Marchais Center.

The elephant staircase.

Virtually unknown to many natives of both Manhattan and Staten Island, this museum is unique in its tranquil setting and its collections of Tibetan religious art and volumes related to the teachings of Buddha. The entrance, on a shady country street, is marked by a tiny sign that simply says "Tibetan Art." You ring the bell, and a woman comes upstairs. From her string of keys she unlocks the chain across the door. The woman is Helen Anglade Watkins, who runs the museum. Usually, small children are discouraged from entering because the gardens are built on steep cliffs and are carefully landscaped.

In the gardens, set along niches in the walls or at the stairs, are stone sculptures of squirrels, rabbits, snakes, lizards, frogs, sacred monkeys, and elephants. There are a lotus pool, charming birdhouses, a wishing well, leaf-hidden life-size Buddhas, and cast-iron garden benches with floral and leaf designs.

The Center was built by Jacques Marchais, the professional name of Mrs. Harry Klauber, for ten years a dealer in Oriental art. Mrs. Klauber died in 1948. The museum contains her collection of Oriental Buddhist art. Helen Anglade Watkins, executrix of the estate, operates the museum as a memorial to Mrs. Klauber, as provided under the will of Mr. Klauber, who died eight months after his wife.

| 303

*Examples of
fine Tibetan art.*

The three-acre, hilltop museum has three main sections: the library, the lamasery altar, and the landscaped grounds. The library, containing all of Mrs. Klauber's books, is furnished with massive, elaborately carved, red-lacquered Chinese furniture. The books are all in English and are intended to serve as a library on the Orient for students. There are no original manuscripts, but there are many books about Tibet, Buddhism, Asian art, and on perfumes, gems, and colors as applied to Tibetan art, as well as a complete set of source books on where to find the "Sacred Books of the East."

The skylit main building has the shape of a Tibetan temple, with an authentic lamasery altar of granite blocks in three tiers. On the shelves are scores of gold, silver, and bronze idols of various Buddhist sects of Tibet and India, China and Japan. Helen Watkins describes the religious objects, and introduces the visitor to the melodious nara gong, shaped like a huge brass soup pot.

The altar is intended to re-create a Tibetan altar as closely as possible. It is ornate and crowded with hand prayer wheels, incense burners, vases, masks used in religious plays, one-note, metallic-sounding horns used to call the monks into the temple, offering bowls, intricately carved and gilded wooden statuettes of Buddhist deities, and votive altar tablets. Many of the Buddha images bear white scarves, brought here as a mark of reverence by the monks who live in a Buddhist monastery nearby in New Jersey. Many interesting wall banners, or tankas, made by lamas depict stories of various teachers and deities. Opposite the altar wall squats a heroic-sized Chinese Buddha dating from about 1700.

The Jacques Marchais Center is a replica of a Tibetan temple for meditation and inspiration. Images in the museum were fashioned according to regulations in the sacred books.

The Tibetan collection also displays calligraphic wooden blocks; robes; heavy silver skull bowls studded with turquoise and coral, which are used for offerings; Tibetan butter containers from which the lamas replenish their lamps; aprons of carved human bones used by priests in necromantic rites, and hundreds of other objects of Buddhist art.

THE RICHMONDTOWN RESTORATION

Address: Arthur Kill and Richmond Roads, Richmondtown, Staten Island, N.Y.
Phone: 351-1611

Days: Daily, 2–5; Sundays, 2–6. Closed Mondays (museum). For other buildings, inquire at museum desk.
Admission: Free.

Subway: IRT 7th Ave. or IRT Lexington Ave. to South Ferry, then take Staten Island Ferry (5¢) to St. George.
Bus: From St. George take bus #113, or #108 to Richmondtown.
Auto: (1) From St. George left along Bay St., right to Victory Blvd., left at St. Paul's. Continue on same road as name changes to Van Duzer, then Richmond Road. Follow road to its end. (2) From Verrazano Bridge: Richmond Road exit, follow road to its end. Ample street parking.

Gift Shop: Sales counter in Historical Museum has candy, small souvenirs, and publications for sale.

| 305

Museum Memberships: From $5.00 annual membership to $1,000.00 as patron member. Members receive monthly publication.

Library: Books, documents, and photographs about Staten Island.

Staten Island Historical Society.

The Richmondtown Restoration is a project New Yorkers can be proud of. It incorporates in a small village some of the finest examples of historical architecture and artifacts on public view in New York. The Restoration expresses the courage and determination of a community to preserve its heritage.

Richmondtown is a community-sponsored project. The City of New York has promised to match all privately donated funds, but since large foundations do not want to allocate funds without assuming some control of the project no donation large enough to ensure the finish of the project has yet come in. Many in the project are volunteers.

When all the elements are complete, the Restoration will contain the following units: Schoolhouse, General Store, Historical Museum, Blacksmith Shop, Wagon Sheds, Law Office, Town Jail, Court Houses, Town Houses, Country Houses, Cottages, Farms, Barns, Mill House, Town Bridge, Cooper's Shop, Basketmaker's Shop, Tavern, Church-yard—about thirty buildings that will show the evolution of an American village through the seventeenth, eighteenth, and nineteenth centuries.

The earliest mention of the village was in 1700, when the settlement was referred to as "Cocklestown," because of the oyster and clam shells, or cockles, that were found nearby. After the Revolution, Richmondtown was its accepted name. Growth of the village was dependent on its function as the county seat. When Staten Island became part of the city in 1898, Richmondtown was abandoned as the county seat, and lost its primary incentive for growth. Building was at a standstill from then on; and since there had been little change in the topography of the area since the seventeenth century, historians found it an ideal site for restoration.

An outstanding building in the village is the Voorlezer House, the oldest known elementary-school building in the United States. It was built for the Dutch Church congregation before 1696. "Voorlezer" derives from the Dutch word for "fore-reader," a title given to laymen who taught school and read church services. The Voorlezer also lived in the building.

This quaint, two-story clapboard Dutch-Colonial is higher in front than in back, which gives the roof and the building a lopsided look. The foundation walls are two feet thick, and the timbers in the building are of solid oak. The floorboards are white pine, sixteen inches wide.

In the downstairs room with its large open fireplace, services were

Voorlezer House.

held. Upstairs were a bedchamber and probably the schoolroom. Of special note are the broad, uneven ax marks left in the garret by the primitive housebuilders. Although the schoolhouse is furnished with present-day copies of eighteenth-century school furnishings, the Voorlezer House is nevertheless a distinguished National Historical landmark.

The Samuel Grosset House (Treasure House) was erected on its present site near the Mill Pond and St. Andrew's Church in 1700. Grosset, a tanner, later sold the land with tan vats, yards, curing pits, hides and leather to another tanner. After the Revolutionary War, $7,000 in gold was found hidden in the walls of the house, and it is believed the building may have been used as a paymaster's office.

St. Andrew's Church, founded in 1708, and its historic graveyard are separated from the Restoration by Mill Pond stream. The oldest gravestone is in memory of Sibbel Arnol, who died in 1742 at the age of four. Her father was rector of St. Andrew's from 1740–1745.

Third County Courthouse.

The Guyon-Lake-Tysen House was built about 1740 by Joseph Guyon. His name is etched over the dining-room door. In the 1800's the Lake family came into possession of the property, and intermarried with the Tysens. The kitchen is considered the earliest portion of the building, and may have formed Guyon's entire house. It has double Dutch doors.

Stephen's General Store, established in 1837, displays a complete post office with pigeonholes, two potbelly stoves, pottery from Bennington, Vermont, and upstate New York, captain's chairs, decorated tinware for flour, sugar, and tea. The shelves carry patent medicines, tobacco tins, innumerable small household items, rolling pins, ladles, and coffee grinders. From the ceiling hang birdcages, oil lamps, baskets, ice skates, huge tin pitchers, ancient scales—all creating a comfortable country-store atmosphere.

The Newspaper Office offers a glimpse of a small-town printing office with a hand-operated typeset and printing press. One wall is full of cowhide-bound books.

The imposing Greek Revival building at the Center Street intersection is the Third County Courthouse, dating from 1837. It has a volunteer firemen's exhibit and a sportsmen's room with hand-carved

Inside the Staten Island Historical Society.

Stephen's Country Store.

waterfowl decoys for sea gulls, black-breasted plovers, dowitches, pintails, mallards, Canadian geese, and whistling swans, an unusual collection. The fire-fighting exhibit contains an old-time fire wagon and some minor paraphernalia related to local volunteer firemen—medals, horns, photographs, and decorated belts. The building is open only on Sundays, from two to five.

The Staten Island Historical Society Museum is the keystone of the Restoration. It occupies the County Clerk and Surrogate's Office built in 1848. Many of the cast-iron doors remain. Prints, drawings, broadsides, and colored lithographs show early scenes of Staten Island. There is a modest group of post-office patriotic Civil War covers and other post-office canceled letters from 1818–1900. The Elliott Burgher Commemorative Pitcher Collection contains luster, Staffordshire, and Liverpool ware dating from 1785 to 1835, and depicting the landing of the Pilgrims, Cornwallis's surrender, the opening of the Erie Canal, and the Battle of Waterloo.

The lower floor also has household effects, coffee grinders, utensils, baking dishes, old sewing machines, pewterware, rare Victorian laundry equipment for washing, wringing, scrubbing, and mangling clothes and, for the finishing touches, the Edward Menden Collection of hand pressing irons used for collars, cuffs, and ruffles. There are also tin candle makers, spinning wheels, looms, butter churners, blacksmith equipment, and a comprehensive collection of hardware and tools for barrelmakers, wagonmakers, and shoemakers, ranging from clamps, gauges, saws, drills, chisels, braces, mallets—all of which have a vague connection with some of the handyman tools we use today.

The upper floor of the museum has an open balcony with an interesting group of photographs showing historic houses of Staten Island as they were in the late 1800's and early 1900's. Some of the Richmondtown Restoration buildings are in this group. Some have disappeared entirely.

In a glass case is a copy of Milton's *Paradise Lost* printed in Dutch in 1691. There is also a group of relics of the Revolution recovered from the British camps in Richmondtown—handmade buttons, belt buckles, and copper pennies. An antique doctor's kit contains an instrument used for bleeding, old hacksaws, and a case of small pills, all the same size and color.

A toy room displays tin soldiers, dollhouses, puzzles, penny banks, china dolls, trains, and miniature furniture of the 1880's.

Excavating the jail site.

CONFERENCE HOUSE

Address: South end of Hylan Blvd., Staten Island, N.Y.
Phone: YU 4-2086

Days: Open daily, 10–5; Oct. 1st to April 1st, 10–4. Closed Mondays.
Admission: $.25. Free Tuesday and Thursday. Children free if accompanied by a parent or teacher.

Subway: IRT 7th Ave. or IRT Lexington Ave. to South Ferry, then take Staten Island Ferry (5¢) to St. George.
Bus: From St. George take bus #103 to Craig Ave.
Train: From St. George ferry dock on Staten Island take rapid transit to Tottenville. From Bentley St. turn right onto Craig St., and right again at Hylan Blvd.
Auto: (1) From St. George turn left onto Bay St.; then right at Canal St. Note that street name changes to Tompkins Blvd., then Hylan Blvd. Follow Hylan Blvd. to its end. (2) From Verrazano Bridge take Hylan Blvd. exit south. Follow Hylan Blvd. to its end. Ample street parking.

Food: Ice-cream and soda vendors are stationed at end of Hylan Blvd. most afternoons.

Membership: Conference House Association invites members. $2.00 annual dues maintain building and provide resident caretaker.

The Conference House at the tip of Staten Island gives the impression that almost nothing in and about the house has changed since the building was built in the late 1680's. This section of the island is still beautifully rural. Present-day reality intrudes only in the Sunday congregation of families and couples sprawled in camp chairs and on blankets on the wide lawn that slopes gently down to the sandy shore of the Raritan River. From time to time white sails drift by. There is perhaps no better way to enjoy history.

312 | Inside Conference House is an 1850 lithograph showing the house from across the river. Its legend says that on this location the scenery, fishing, bathing, springs, and "salubriety" stand unrivaled; this is the most beautiful and romantic spot in New York.

Considering that the house was built before 1687, it is remarkable how well preserved its architectural features are. Except for the re-

Conference House.

moval of a high porch, the exterior has changed little. Interior rooms have the original wide-board floors and exposed-beam ceilings.

The right parlor on the first floor is sparsely furnished. It contains some chairs and an inlaid tilt-top table given to John Adams by Lafayette. It is in the dining room on the left that the historic conference giving the house its name was held. A set of iron kettles and cooking pots hang in the huge cellar fireplace. The exposed rough stones are particularly attractive, and show what pioneer builders could do with raw materials. There is also a thirty-foot vault that may have been used as a dungeon.

In the bedrooms upstairs are many chairs and cribs. A small cubicle contains dozens of Indian arrowheads collected around the property. In this small room Christopher Billopp is supposed to have killed one of his slave girls in a fit of violence.

Thomas Billopp, a captain in the British Navy who built the house, came to America in 1674. He received a grant from the Honorable Thomas Dongan, Governor-General of all his Royal Highness's territory in America, for the Manor of Bentley in 1687. Bentley was the post-office address until 1861, when it was changed to Tottenville. Billopp roamed the seas, and died in England in 1725.

His second daughter, Anne, married Thomas Farmer. Their third son, Thomas Farmer, Jr., born in 1711, inherited the manor from his grandfather. Under the provisions of the will he changed his name to Thomas Billopp. His gravestone is in the underground vault in the cellar.

His oldest son, Colonel Christopher Billopp, born in 1737, lived in the house until the close of the Revolution. Then he, along with other British sympathizers, moved to St. John, New Brunswick, and the Billopp mansion was confiscated.

Lord Howe took possession of Staten Island for the British on July 4, 1776. He soon requested a meeting with a delegation from the colonists to discuss possible peace terms to end the war. On September 11, 1776, a committee consisting of Benjamin Franklin, John Adams, and Edward Rutledge met with Lord Howe at the Billopp Mansion. The delegates for the colonists declined every proposal that would compromise the Declaration of Independence that had been signed only weeks earlier. When peace did come, it is sig-

A battery of useful pots.

A perfect view of the Raritan River.

nificant that the terms followed those outlined by the colonists at this first, historic peace conference.

Since the Revolution a number of different owners have lived in Conference House. As early as 1846 a historian suggested that the building be preserved. In October, 1918, the Gillespie Powder plant across the river exploded and broke all the windows in the Billopp Mansion. The tenants then moved out, and thus for the only time in its long history the mansion was uninhabited for the next two years. It was during this time that "much was damaged by some of the savages of civilization." Finally, in 1926, a real-estate corporation purchased the estate and generously gave the house and grounds to the city with the stipulation that they be preserved as a museum and park.

Alphabetical List of Museums